Chuen King Lecture Series

General Editor : Lung-kwong LO

1. *Jesus, Paul and John* (1999)
   by C. K. Barrett, A. J. Malherbe, Kosuke Koyama

2. *Reading, Studying and Interpreting the Bible*
   (In Chinese, 2000) by Daniel Chow, James Cheung, Eric Wong, Simon Wong et al.

3. *Gospel Writing and Church Politics: A Socio-rhetorical Approach* (2001)
   by Gerd Theissen

4. *Hebrew Origins* (2002)
   by Jack M. Sasson

5. *Endings* (In Chinese, forthcoming)
   by Morna Hooker

Chuen King Lecture Series 4

HEBREW ORIGINS
Historiography
History
Faith of Ancient Israel

Jack M. Sasson
with comments by Archie C.C. Lee,
Craig Y. S. Ho and Fook Kong Wong

Theology Division, CHUNG CHI COLLEGE, CUHK
HONG KONG 2002

Hebrew Origins

Author	: Jack M. Sasson
Respondents	: Archie C. C. Lee, Craig Y. S. Ho, Fook Kong Wong
Publisher	: Theology Division, Chung Chi College, The Chinese University of Hong Kong, Shatin, New Territories, Hong Kong.
Editor	: Lung-Kwong Lo
Assistant Editors	: Peony O. S. Cheung, Clement C. H. Chan
Telephone	: (852) 2609 6705
Fax	: (852) 2603 5224
Email	: theology@cuhk.edu.hk
Website	: www.cuhk.edu.hk/theology/
Design and Production	: Wise & Wide Design & Printing Co. Ltd. (852) 2558 7800

First Edition, November 2002, Hong Kong

©2002 Theology Division, Chung Chi College,
The Chinese University of Hong Kong

ISBN: 962-7137-25-1

Printed in Hong Kong

Contents

Contents

Editor's Preface

" Chuen King" in Chinese literally means "communicating scripture" (傳經). This is the name of the lectureship which is established in memory of Mr. Wong Chuen-king by his son Mr. Wong Bing-lai who believes in the power of biblical message. While the Bible is the primary source for Christian theology, it also witnesses the process of contextualizing the Word of God in different ages and among different people. Today in Asian churches, including Chinese Christian communities, one of the main concerns is to contextualize Christian theologies, which have been developed in the West for almost two thousand years, in their own contexts.

There are different approaches in dealing with the issue of contextualization, however, no one can do contextual theology without biblical resources. As a matter of fact, the Bible is the common basis for the faith of all Christians in different contexts. Thus, one of the most important starting points of doing contextual theology is no doubt the study of the Bible. What concerns us most in biblical studies is to understand the text in its original context and the second thing that is of concern to us is how the text should be interpreted in our contemporary contexts. The Chuen King Lectureship aims to promote biblical studies in these two perspectives. We believe that we can learn from western biblical scholars on their studies of what the Scripture meant in its original contexts, but we must also work hard to understand the messages in our own contexts.

Editor's Preface

Chuen King Lectureship has been organized since 1996. We have invited renowned biblical scholars and theologians to share their insights and findings. We are delighted to have Prof. Abraham Malherbe of Yale University and Prof. C. K. Barrett of Durham University to be our speakers to kick off the Lectureship in 1996 and Prof. Kosuke Koyama of Union Theological Seminary, New York, former Dean of South-east Asia Graduate School of Theology and a forerunner of Asian theologies, to be our lecturer in 1997. Their lectures were published in both English and Chinese in the book *Jesus, Paul and John* (1999). In January 1999, sixteen young Chinese scholars from different seminaries and universities in Hong Kong jointly conducted seminars and gave lectures on the topic of *Reading, Studying and Interpreting the Bible*. Their manuscripts in Chinese were published. In February 2000, we were delighted to have Prof. Gerd Theissen of Heidelberg University to deliver the Fourth Chuen King Lecture on *Gospel Writing and Church Politics*. The revised and expanded version of the Lecture was published in May 2001, the Spanish and Korean translations of which were published in 2002.

All the previous Chuen King Lectures have focused on the New Testament. This may have given the impression that we are more interested in studying this part of the Bible, but in fact this is not the case. In February of 2001, we were so delighted to have Prof. Jack M. Sasson of Vanderbilt University to deliver the Fifth Chuen King Lecture on *Hebrew Origins*. Prof. Sasson is gifted in making sophisticated issues interesting and comprehensible even for non-academics. He sustained the interest of the audience throughout, and, the lectures and discussions were followed by an actively engaged questions and answers section.

The origins of Hebrew, comparable to that of Chinese, were diverse and mysterious. Both races shared many similarities: long history, dispersion of their people all over the world, and their pragmatic characters to face up to hardships. However, there is a major difference when it comes to studying their origins. Methodologies to study the origins of Hebrew have been well developed while there is much less for the Chinese. It is therefore crucial for the Chinese to work diligently to understand their origins and cultures of the past. To learn the origins of Hebrew and Chinese are important for Chinese Christians to understand their identity and to construct their theology. The contribution of Prof. Sasson's lectures and this book will have a continued impact on them.

In order to start a dialogue between Prof. Sasson's work and the Christians in Hong Kong, we invited three Old Testament scholars who received their doctoral degrees from the West to give their initial responses during the Lecture. We are grateful for their willingness to participate in and to provide us with the written text which we have happily included at the end of each chapter in this book. Their views provided a good starting point for this dialogue to take place which is crucial for us to contextualize the findings of western scholars. Hence, we will not only publish this book in English but will also translate and publish it in Chinese.

Prof. Sasson was so serious about this book that he revised the lectures after he returned to Nashville. We are much indebted to his labour and friendship. The memories of the time Prof. and Mrs. Sasson spent with us is still very fresh in our mind. We look forward to their next visit and the opportunities to get more insights from them again.

In preparing this book, we are grateful to the timely assistance from our research student Mr. Chi-ho Chan. He has helped us in proof reading and ensuring that the Hebrew characters remain intact in the course of production. Mr. Chan is also responsible for preparing the general index. The effort of Ms. Peony Oi-sze Cheung in editing and administrating the various aspects relating to the publication is also appreciated.

May God bless all who are involved in making the publication of this book possible and continue to endow His richest blessings upon all who are working so hard to contextualize Christian theologies.

LO, Lung-kwong (Rev. Prof.)
Head, Theology Division
Chung Chi College, CUHK
November, 2002

FOREWORD

When Professor Lo Lung-Kwong invited me to deliver a series of lectures in Hong Kong, I naturally asked him about my audience. Although an Asian by birth (in Aleppo, Syria), I had not yet set foot in the Far East and had only virtual knowledge (through the media, books, and food) of its culture. The audience, Dr. Lo assured me, would not be too different from what I encounter whenever I lecture in America: knowledgeable, but not necessarily scholarly; interested, but not there to be bored; committed to its faith, but not beyond welcoming new insights on the origins of that faith.

I offered Dr. Lo three lectures on Hebrew Origins. Strange as it may seem given the popularity of the theme in scholarly and popular literature, the title has been used (as far as I know) only once previously. In 1936, Theophile James Meek produced a nice book out of the 1933–34 Haskell Lectures he was invited to deliver at the Graduate School of Theology, Oberlin College. The lectures were extensively rewritten for the published volume, *Hebrew Origins* (NY: Harper and Brothers). I know of the book only in its third, extensively revised, Harper Torchbooks edition (1960), and it seemed to me that some of the issues he raised could bear revisit, especially by someone who sits at Vanderbilt University, whose Divinity School merged with the now defunct Oberlin GST in 1966, the year Meek died. But there was no question of investigating the same ground that Meek covered in six chapters: the origins of the Hebrew people, laws, God, priesthood, prophecy, and Monotheism.

Born in 1881, Meek trained as an Assyriologist but wrote best on Hebraic culture. He was a fine philologian and a committed historian, for whom the alliance between archaeology and the recovered document was a path to the reconstruction of the true past. His pages rarely displayed hesitance, his perspective was encyclopedic, his opinions well founded for their time. Meek was writing in an age that was buoyed by the extensive archival discoveries at, among other sites, Nuzi, Ugarit, and Mari. The light their texts shed on the second millennium BCE promised to also bring the origin of the Hebrews out of the darkness that had enveloped it since time immemorial.

The lectures I give below will display little of that certitude about diverse aspects of Hebrew origins, even if, at least superficially, I share the same interest as Meek (Assyriology and Bible). No doubt our knowledge of the past has improved; but as it will be made amply clear from the lectures, this increase of knowledge has also broadened the limits of our ignorance and rattled our confidence in the possibility of making texts and artifacts reveal their secrets. Typical of this condition is that my initial lecture focused on Hebrew historiography, a subject that earned scant paragraphs in Meek's book.

The lectures I delivered in Hong Kong (and repeated in Taipei) during those magic days of February 2001 are more or less what you will read below. The third lecture, however, has been reshaped (I hope with some success) to take into accounts responses made by my audience and by colleagues. I have added footnotes to the whole and have appended a bibliography that might proof useful for those who wish to follow up on issues I have raised. There, I have preferred citing readable, relatively brief, articles in recent reference sets rather than studies in difficult to access journals. At all times, even when I offered controversial or debatable opinions, I have kept in mind that these lectures addressed a discerning audience rather than biblical specialists. Let me warn, however, that I have used CE and BCE, when AD and BC are more familiar to most readers and that I have not always succeeded to avoid gendering the Hebrew God, when a major point I make is that the ancient Hebrews did not attribute sexuality and gender to that God.

I am very grateful for the incredible hospitality I met in Hong Kong, Guangzhou, and Taipei. As one who has organized lectures, I know how immense is the outlay of energy and time to make them work. Dr. Lo Lung-Kwong will remain for me (and for my wife Diane) the paradigmatic host, and the army of colleagues and staff that participated in our visit has earned our gratitude. In Hong Kong, there were Peony Oi-sze Cheung and Tracy Chan to make sure that nothing went awry, but also the admirable Joseph Kaung who, for the duration, became so successfully my mouthpiece that on occasions I thought myself speaking Cantonese or Mandarin. I must not fail also to extend warm thanks to colleagues who honored me by responding to my remarks: Dr. Archie Lee, Dr. Wong Fook Kong, and Dr. Ho Craig Yuet Shun. Ms. Cheung and Clement C. H. Chan assisted Dr. Lo in editing the manuscript, and I am pleased to thank them all for their effort.

I should also take this occasion to thank Dr. Lin Hong-Hsin of the Taiwan Theological College and Seminary, where the series of lectures was also delivered. There, I was flattered by the responses of Drs Chen Ching-Wen, Tsan Tsong-Sheng, and John Wu. Dr. Janet Su ably translated my words. In Guangzhou's South China Normal University, Ms. He Zhangrong and Dr. Lin Zhongze ably hosted my wife and me.

I must not end without giving due credit to Dr. Wong Bing Lai who, in dedicating the lecture series to the memory of his father, Mr. Wong Chuen King, made it possible for East and West to share knowledge of faith traditions that, albeit born centuries ago, continue to give humanity dignity and hope.

Jack M. Sasson
May, 2002

FIRST LECTURE

History as Literature in
Ancient Israel

FIRST LECTURE
HISTORY AS LITERATURE IN
ANCIENT ISRAEL

A. CONTEXT AND BACKGROUND
1. The End of the Ancient Near East

In August 70 CE, troops led by the future Roman emperor Titus destroyed the Third Temple, which King Herod had completed only a few decades earlier. The destruction was complete. There were attempts to rebuild it by Julian the Apostate around 364 AD and again when Persians controlled Jerusalem for a very brief interval during the Byzantine period (early in the seventh century). By then, however, the culture that was known to us from the Hebrew Bible had undergone transformation. In its place, two young religions, Judaism and Christianity, both daughters of the Hebrew faith, were born, emerging from the same social upheavals and eschatological yearnings that were gripping the area when the temple was destroyed under Roman rule. Jewish sages developed laws of *kashruth* (dietary observances) by adapting and enjoining on all Jews, regardless of class and gender, the cult services that had formerly taken place in the destroyed temple. Synagogues, a place for prayers in the diaspora but only for discussing the Torah in Palestine itself, became increasingly central to the religious experience as Jews became increasingly aware that the temple was not to be rebuilt anytime soon.[1] Early Christianity allegorized in Christ's passion

---

[1] A fine overview of Judaism from the 2nd century BCE (BC) to the 2nd century CE (AD) is Cohen 1987. His comments on the evolution of the Synagogue are on pp. 111-116.

the temple sacrificial rituals, making unnecessary the reconstruction of the temple.

About the time the Romans destroyed Jerusalem in 70 AD, in Mesopotamia, a scribe was copying the last tablets to be written in cuneiform. Soon afterwards there would be no scribes who could read the vast number of documents written in that script. Mesopotamian monuments quickly became curiosities and their messages were lost. In Egypt, the hieroglyphic script had ceased to function as an instrument for communication in the Ptolemaic period, the Coptic script replacing it. Although it continued to be used by a very small circle of priests until the fourth century, the vast amount of information and knowledge that hieroglyphics had transmitted during the three millennia was quickly becoming lost. For centuries afterwards the curious interpreted symbolically the nice pictures carved on ancient walls.[2]

2. The Survival of the Bible

The Bible itself was never forgotten. When the Jerusalem temple was destroyed in the first century, a number of versions of the Bible were widely circulating, two of which had significant differences. There was a Hebrew version, but there was also a version in Greek that was appreciably larger, containing a number of books not in the Hebrew version. Soon there were also versions

---

[2]   For the last cuneiform text, see Sachs 1976. By the Hellenistic period, hieroglyphics had become so esoteric that few scribes knew how to read them; those that did were using them cryptographically. The latest document written in Hieroglyphics is dated to 394 CE; see Goldwasser 2001.

in Aramaic, but these generally depended on the Hebrew or Greek. While Jews found it attractive to hear and read their holy texts in contemporaneous languages, such as Aramaic, Greek, and Latin, learned men and scribes kept alive the Hebrew version, which they presumed to be original, in the sense that this was the account that was received in Sinai, and that inspired prophets and sages. Christians relied on the Greek version, translating it first into Latin. The Hebrew version was comprehensible to few Christians until the reformation, when its contents once more become vital.

3. The Survival of the ANE through the Bible

By the fourth century CE, Christianity was triumphing all over the Near East and in the next few centuries it would also triumph in Europe. While in the seventh century Islam wrested away a good portion of the Near East, knowledge of the past for both Jews and Christians was primarily limited to the information found in the Bible. Naturally, for both Jews and Christians there was never a question about the veracity of the Bible. The Bible was taken to be the holy word of God, as transmitted through his faithful servants. Still, if there was any curiosity about the nations and cultures that were contemporary with the patriarchs, the kings, and prophets of Israel, it could not be fulfilled because knowledge of their script had disappeared. Besides, these foreign cultures were pagan, and anything that they might have revealed would not have been trusted.

4. The Rediscovery of the Ancient Near East

I must reserve for another occasion the story of how and why there came to be an interest in rediscovering the ancient world.[3] The reassessment of the culture of ancient Israel in light of the resurrection of the Ancient Near East is a passionate story that draws on many sources. It involves reliance on tools first invented by Arab grammarians to better appreciate what the Hebrew Bible had to say. It draws upon the recovery of the classical heritage that made Europeans appreciate the rich cultures contemporaneous with the Hebrews. It was fostered by the rise of Protestantism with its allegiance to the original meaning of the Hebrew Bible and enhanced by the eclipse of a fourfold interpretation of sacred scripture (literal, allegorical, moral, and mystical). And it depended upon the development of analytical tools (beginning in the 18th century) with which to assess history, including the history of Israel.

But for our purpose, nothing was quite as significant as the clash of cultures that occurred when, in the nineteenth century, Europe was ready to test itself against Middle Eastern powers, something it had not done since the Crusade. The dominance was not political this time around, but cultural, and moral. Europeans did not set out to occupy land, although they eventually did; rather they sought to spread their culture and, they hoped, their religion through trade, missions, and schools. Among those who were sent to the Middle East were archaeologists, at first

---

[3] Some nice articles on this topic are assembled in volume 1 of Sasson 1995, Part I, "The Ancient near East in Western Thought."

mostly looters, who took back monuments written in hieroglyphics and cuneiform. When, by a miracle that is still difficult to understand, they deciphered the obtuse texts, the hunger that was produced for more knowledge of the past and for better means to know about Israel and could not be satisfied.[4]

There was a signal moment on December 3, 1872. George Smith, a man who taught himself how to read cuneiform, gave a lecture before the Society of Biblical Archaeology, with Gladstone, the British Prime Minister, in the audience. Smith revealed his discovery of a tablet that explained how a Mesopotamian named Utnapishtim survived a Flood the gods had sent to destroy humankind. The story sounded very much like the story of Noah in the book of Genesis. At the time, it was believed that it antedated the Hebrew version of the Flood. In fact, while other versions of the Flood story from Mesopotamia were crafted centuries before the one Smith read, the Hebrew account (itself made of two intertwined variants) was practically coeval with it (G. Smith, 1874).

The news was sensational, because it implied that Sacred Scripture was itself copied from pagan stories. This possibility could cast doubt on the divine inspiration of Hebrew narratives. Similar discoveries, for example that of the "Code" of Hammurabi at the end of the century, spurred the west to excavate deeper all over the ancient world. The result was a wave of spectacular

---

[4] The story of the decipherment has been told often; see most recently in Pope 1999. A briefer accounting is Daniels 1995.

discoveries of monuments and archives that not only provided us with information about the cultures among which Israel developed, but also forced us to inspect the Biblical text in search of its meaning, goals, and conventions. Without these developments, these lectures would not be conceivable.

B. CONTRIBUTION OF RECENT RESEARCH
1. The Bible – How It Came to Be

Despite the incredible amount of scholarship and ingenuity that was showered on the study of the Hebrew and Greek Bibles, we have only conjectures about its origins and compilation. At one time, the largely Protestant and European scholarship developed a hypothesis by which to explain why the biblical text, despite its powerful narrative style, displayed contradictions, non-sequiturs, and duplication. This scholarship suggested that a series of at least four documents, produced in different times, by different circles, and for largely different goals, were eventually stitched together, probably just after the return of the Hebrews from exile in Babylon. The great scholar Julius Wellhausen took these documents (labeled J for the Yahwist, E for the Elohist, D for the Deuteronomist, and P for the Priestly source) and by applying notions derived from contemporaneous research into the development of religious belief, placed them in a sequence from the tenth to the sixth century BCE.[5]

---

[5] The story of the Documentary Hypothesis has been retold often in biblical encyclopedias (Rogerson 1992), in individual chapters (Hayes 1979) and monographs (Clements 1983). See further the comments in the final lecture.

But despite its brilliance, cracks were quickly found in what has been called the *Documentary Hypothesis*. To begin with, the hypothesis did not deal adequately with the testimony from the literature of the ancient Near East. As it was deciphered, this literature displayed similar contradictions and repetitions. It also gave multiple names to each god, without necessarily requiring the fusion of separate documents. For example, the Gilgamesh Epic, in its first millennium version, is a veritable compendium of previous lore that has been reshaped to drive the plot of a tale that, from all evidence, is the creation of a single, albeit anonymous, poet. Additionally, scholars were realizing that literature survives in oral forms for centuries before it is converted into writing. The discoveries of archeological remains from first millennium Israel, and our appreciation of the literary forms of biblical narratives, have compelled us to rethink the formation of the Hebrew Bible. Let us begin by speaking about the Hebrew script.

2. Hebrew Script – The Complications

We now have a sense, but no definite proof, for how the Hebrew alphabet evolved. We know that Hebrews adopted a 22 consonant writing system to record a language that had at least five more phonemes consisting of three consonants that were affected by nearby vowels and two consonants that were represented by symbols with double readings (ḥet and ʿayin). We also know that when they began to use that script, Hebrews did not bother separating different words. Because the early script did not have special symbols for vowels, a line with about 25 consonants and no space between them could be segmented in a great number of ways, yielding radically different meanings for words and phrases.[6] The consequence is that we now have a full industry of scholars who specialize in shifting some consonants from one word to another or making entirely new words from consonants deemed superfluous. It should be clear to you now why there can never be an end to new translations and new commentaries.

3. Hebrew Language – Virtues and Limitations

We have also learned a lot about the Hebrew language and it how it operated. To begin with, we now know that the Hebrew we read with so much care is a composite, an artificial creation. Consonants came from an infinitely earlier period than the vowels, so that what we read is the pronunciation of the language from the time of Christ rather than the Hebrew of the monarchic period. We know from Assyrian and Greek transcriptions that some famous people had names that sounded different from their Hebrew version. For example, Kings Menahem and Jehu of Israel answered to the names "Menihimmu" and "Yaw'a" respectively.[7] Of more consequence, the Masorites, those people who placed vowels under the consonants around 700 CE, did not know that certain verbal forms (for example the *qal* passive) existed, and so vocalized them differently (as *niphal* for the imperfect and as *pual* for the perfect).[8] Occasionally too, some words were punctuated in a way that reflected changing ideologies. For example, the Masorites vocalized the Hebrew word for "fat"(ḥelev) as "milk"

---

[6] On all this, see the convenient article of Lemaire 1992. The book of Würthwein (1979) is full of information on textual matters.
[7] Zadok 1988: 459-465, collects names of Israelites preserved in cuneiform, hieroglyphic, and Greek scripts.
[8] See William 1970; Knauf 1990.

(ḥalav) and so gave us the famous prohibition "You may not cook a kid in its mother's milk" (Exodus 23:19, 34:26; Deuteronomy 14:21) that has contributed very heavily to Jewish dietary laws. The injunction may simply have sensibly urged people not to destroy their flock by cooking a kid in the fat of its slaughtered mother.[9]

We also know that in earlier Hebrew certain consonants that acted as prepositions (for example the consonant "*lamed*") had broader, occasionally even opposite, meanings than we had realized. Thus, a very famous prophetic passage that played a role in Christian historiographies, "And to Zion will come a redeemer ... " (Isaiah 59:20), is now understood by many to translate as, "And *from* Zion will come a redeemer." So when in the gospel of Matthew (2:13–18) we read about the Christ child coming back to Zion after a visit to Egypt, we realize that story was trying to fulfill a prophecy whose real meaning had been lost for centuries.

4. Hebrew Grammar and Hebrew "Anthropology"

Better appreciation of Hebrew, and for that matter, other Semitic languages, has allowed us insight into both the promise and also the limitation of the language. The Hebrew of the Bible is a relatively easy language to learn, having a rather limited vocabulary, a restricted "verbal" system, and a vestigial case declension. It also has no neuter gender. Consequently, if a Hebrew wished to speak of God, his language forced him to use a gender, male or female. When we hear colleagues say that the

---

[9] See Sasson forthcoming[3].

Hebrew treated God as a male and so betrayed a patriarchal perspective, the nature of the Hebrew language robs us from establishing whether in truth the Hebrew personified his God as a male rather than as an abstract, non-gendered deity.

In fact, Hebrew is extremely poor in the vocabulary for the abstract. If a Hebrew prophet wanted to speak of God's compassion or anger, he had to use metaphors that are based on the human anatomy. For example he speaks of God's "womb (via raḥam)" and "burning face (ḥarôn ʾap)." Because of the nature of the language, therefore, it is very difficult to establish whether or not the Hebrews imagined their god in human terms.

Hebrew has a deceptively uncomplicated syntax. Almost all major disputes on understanding what the Hebrew meant have to do with differing opinions on how to appreciate the connection between words. Think of how much is at stake in a proper evaluation of the first verses of Genesis. Here is first, the King James Version:

> In the beginning God created the heaven
> and the earth. And the earth was without form,
> and void; and darkness was upon the face of
> the deep. And the Spirit of God moved upon
> the face of the waters. And God said, Let there
> be light: and there was light...

And here is the Jewish Publication Society's *Tanakh's* version:

When God began to create the heaven and
the earth–the earth being unformed and void,
with darkness over the water God said, let
there be light, and there was light.

The contrast between the two renderings is sharpest in the
way the King James version presents us with a Hebrew God
creating the entire universe out of nothing, a *creatio ex nihilo*. In
the second translation, however, light is the only object that God
creates out of nothing.[10]

C. HEBREW HISTORIOGRAPHY
1. The Medium

In the Near East of antiquity, writing was committed to a wide
variety of material, including stone, wood, clay, skins, and bone.
But there was a tendency to gravitate toward one medium in
each of the regions. For example clay tablets predominated in
Mesopotamia, papyrus in Egypt, a combination of both in Canaan.
This choice of medium had profound consequences on the forms
of the narratives that were recorded. In Mesopotamia scribes
wrote on clay tablets and, but for a few exceptions such as the
Epics of Gilgamesh, Creation, and Erra, generally produced
narratives that could be restricted to one clay table (so as much
as 200 lines). In Egypt papyrus was used. For reasons that are
obscure, Egyptians were reluctant to write literature on papyrus
rolls that were either too high (maximum 8 inches) or too long
(Black and Tait 1995).

---

[10] For the implication of this observation, see the final lecture.

We do not know what the biblical corpus included before it achieved the form known to us today. It is likely that as yet not fully stable versions of all the books we know except for Esther, Daniel, Chronicles, and most of the Apocrypha, were known by the fourth century BCE. In Israel scribes could write on ostraca (shards from clay jars), bones, wooden (waxed or limed) and metal (precious or otherwise) tablets. Literature deemed sacred, however, was written most likely first on papyrus, and then on leather scrolls. These scrolls could attain ten meters and still retain their integrity even after multiple handling. With such a large space, narratives could now trace a single subject over long stretches. Secondary and even tertiary subjects could be accommodated and play important roles in the development of a story that would otherwise not fit on a single sheet or on a clay tablet. Additionally, when these leather scrolls were placed in proximity to each other, the story could be followed for incredibly long intervals. Thus, it requires no imagination for us to posit that something like the narratives now found in the Five Books of Moses and in the Former Prophets (that is Joshua, Judges, Samuel and Kings) must have made sense only if they were placed in sequence, likely early in the fifth century BCE.[11]

2. Narrative Conventions

As collected and edited, the material we call the Bible took the form of a chain of narratives, mostly in prose. To arrive at higher truths, however, poetry could be embedded in it. The story told was of an enduring but troubled relationship between God

---

[11]   See my comments in Sasson, forthcoming[2].

and Israel, the folk he had chosen to be a "light to the nations." According to that narrative, God and Israel did not live in harmony for long. Their vows were often brutally compromised and so required frequent renewal. At the end of the second Book of Kings, the tale ends abruptly, just as Israel was in the midst of another exile, this time not in Egypt, but in Babylon. But by its own reckoning, the story covered more than three millennia and involved dozens of leaders, patriarchs, eponymous ancestors, judges, kings, and prophets. The only constant protagonist in this chain of narratives was God.

In telling this story, certain conventions and literary principles were followed, many of which are common to Semitic narratives. In illustrating some of them, I treat the Biblical text as it reached us rather than as a combination of independent narratives. I also use the term "narrator" when many were surely involved in fashioning or editing the text more or less as we have it now and employ the pronoun "he" when there is no reason to deny that women may have participated in the creative process.

OMNISCIENCE. We notice, first of all, that the narrator is practically always omniscient. By omniscient I mean that the narrator not only knows what is happening, but frequently can penetrate the thoughts of major protagonists, including God. It is amazing that the narrator can report on events before the creation of human beings and can tell why God made a decision to do this and not that. For example, in the account of the Exodus we are told that God hardened the heart of pharaoh, even when this sort of information might draw sympathy to the portrayal of a pharaoh. The narrator can also keep some information from God himself.

For example, in the famous story about the prophet Jonah, the narrator waits until the end of the story (Jonah 4:2) to register Jonah's confession on why he shirked his call to prophecy against Nineveh. The interpretive consequence for keeping this information hidden, from us as well as from God, is enormous. By withholding Jonah's initial reaction to God's directive until after mercy is granted Nineveh, the narrator seriously interferes with the flow of the story. Our own reaction to Jonah, indeed to the whole tale, would surely be quite different had Jonah confessed his doubts about his mission before he headed to Jaffa (Jonah 1: 1-2). In such a reading Jonah, who knows that God will relent, is starkly condescending, so that when God does forgive Nineveh, it would be because there is no other way for God to function; a startling limitation on God's authority.[12]

The narrator can also force a specific interpretation of a story. For example, in telling us about the sacrifice of Isaac, the narrator informs us that God was testing Abraham and so had never intended to allow Isaac's death (Genesis 22). Had the narrator not shared his knowledge of God's intent with us, we might have reacted negatively against a God who would so abuse the only man on earth who had as yet accepted his covenant. (Something similar occurs in Job, when God's scheme is revealed in the opening prose segment.) This entry into God's motivations has its costs, however, for it leaves us to wonder whether other baroque requests of God have similar goals: for example, whether

---

[12]   Sasson 1989: 328-330. On omniscience, see the third chapter of Sternberg 1987. But on this matter, note also the critique of Poland 1988.

God really wished to save Nineveh when conveying a message of doom to a wicked town through a very reluctant prophet, Jonah.

LACK OF DESCRIPTIONS. Another convention is the almost complete lack of description, not just of places and landscape, so important in Greek narratives, but also of physical attributes. This neglect of detail is often accompanied with imprecise information about the age of characters. Such details are left to the reader to fill in, so that each of us may have a different understanding of the context. Thus, it matters enormously how we imagine the scene that occurs when Ruth and Boaz meet on the threshing floor. Whether the reader thinks that she is older or younger than he is, and by how much, can determine how we assess what occurred that night under the stars of Bethlehem.

PLAYS ON WORDS. The Hebrew narrator depended on a number of tricks to advance a story. It can be disconcerting to those who read Scripture in Hebrew to discover how many weighty issues are built around puns on words or even the sound of words. In the story of Adam and Eve, the crafty nature of the snake, said to be ʿarûm, and the naked pair, said to ʿarûmmîm, is driven by a pun. The competition between Isaac's children is sharpened by Jacob's taking from Esau the bĕkōrâ, the right of firstborn, and the bĕrākâ, acquiring a father's blessing. Narratives often depend on cue names that reveal a character's destiny. For example Abel, who gets murdered by Cain, has a name that means "wispiness, vapor." Jacob's name means "the supplanted," and David's name means "beloved." In some cases, the names betray manipulation of traditions. For example, the language in the story of Samuel's birth (1 Samuel 1) is full of references and plays on the Hebrew verbal root šāʾal, meaning "to ask," suggesting that the original version meant to report not on the birth of the prophet Samuel, whose name means something like "El is the Name," but on that of the first king of Israel, Saul, because his name šāʾûl means "requested."[13]

AMORITE CONVENTIONS. Recent scholarship has noted many other narrative conventions that are displayed in Hebrew Scripture. Interestingly, I have found many of these conventions in the letters found at Mari, letters exchanged among Amorites of the early second millennium BCE. As we shall see in the next lecture, the Amorites were of the same stock as the Hebrews. So we can imagine that the artistry of story telling may have been transmitted from generation to another long before Israel was born as a nation.[14]

3. Historiographic Principles

In Israel, the understanding of a narrative was dependent on the reader's recognition and appreciation of paradigms and patterns. These patterns are embedded in a narrative that covers long stretches of time. A number of principles operate in Scripture to create narrative continuity:

---

[13] Alter (1981) offers a fine introduction to these topics; on play on words see, conveniently, Sasson 1976.

[14] Sasson 1998; see also the second lecture.

a. That there is one God who works out his will through one people. From this principle it follows that God is the major and constant character of this epic tale. (See the lecture III in this book.)

b. That during a forty-year sojourn in the desert of Sinai God established his covenant with his people and gave them all the laws that and codes of behavior they will ever need;[15]

c. That success and failure of national endeavors are a measure of that God's approval or disapproval of this people; and

d. That this God guides his people through leaders, one at a time, and that the leader's behavior can be a model for the people; this last principle leads to a focus on biography in the Hebrew scripture.

D. THE BIOGRAPHIC MODE IN HEBREW HISTORIOGRAPHY

Using these guidelines, conventions, and principles, the Hebrews narrated the story of their people. The narrator was guided by a notion, favored in recent centuries by Thomas Carlyle, that "history is the essence of innumerable biographies." His vision was encyclopedic and the subject of his biographies acquired character and purpose from events and goals that occurred centuries later. Consequently, the subjects of the biographies often foreshadow characters that are to follow and their goals are renewed in subsequent narratives. The narrator's vision was also kaleidoscopic: fragments from one biography could be replayed in another. Although the Hebrew crafted biographies in a number

---

[15]   It remains noticeable that Israel is unique in making moral and cultic regulations part of its legal compilations.

of styles, I want to discuss only the two that are most prominent: the episodic biography and the melodramatic biography.[16]

1. The Episodic Biography: The Story of Abram/Abraham

The most prominent example of the episodic biography is the story of Abraham. It is made up of a series of tableaus, each of which is complete in itself. No information from one episode is crucial to appreciating the denouement of another. More important, the episodic biography is structured disjunctively; that is, the full account is discordant in the sequence of scenes that alternate between tension and relaxation, merriment and pathos, piety and religious obstinacy. Furthermore, this sequencing is artificially chronological, with the possibility of shifting, shuffling, and even skipping scenes without incurring serious damage to the final portrait. There is hardly any linkage between and between scenes and cause and effect can rarely be traced among the various *tableaux*.

In each of the tableaus, the subject of the episodic biography remains monochromatic to sharpen the nature of the character within each scene. The emotional range of the hero is, therefore, sharply circumscribed, with introspection and inner enlightenment rarely in evidence. Each scene, however, will reveal a different manifestation of that character, so that, when the series of *tableaux* about one individual is complete, the hero's portrait will emerge as the sum total of his virtues and failings. For theological reasons

---

[16]   For a fuller elaboration, see Sasson 1984.

the biography of Abraham divides into scenes involving Abram and those involving Abraham, so the narrator found it opportune to *repeat*, with important variation, certain settings. It is in this type of biography that we find type-scenes repeating themselves across Hebrew narratives, such as those in which the hero claims to be the brother of his wife (Genesis 12, 16, 20) and those in which a bride is found around a well (Genesis 24, 29, Exodus 2). In the biography, Abraham is cunning and resourceful in Genesis chapters 12 and 20; he trusts his wife to make short-range decisions about his progeny in 16 and 18; he is magnanimous toward Lot in 13 and 18. Other scenes, spread out over the entire portraiture, offer different characterizations: he is warlike and politically shrewd in chapter 14; he is spiritual if not mystical in chapter 15; obedient in chapter 17; he gambles in 22; he is duped in 23; and he is decisive in the early verses of 24. [Table 1.]

	Abram (age)	Abraham (age)
Election & Promise	12:1-9 (75)	17 Circumcision (99) 18 Divine visit
[Wife-sister 1]	12:10-20 Egypt	
Division of land (Lot)	13	19 Sodom & Gomorrah Lot's daughters
[Wife-sister 2]		20 Gerar
Battle with kings	14	
Melchizedek episode	14:18-24	
Covenant	15	21:1-7 Isaac's birth (100)
Hagar & Ishmael	16 (86)	21:8-21 Expulsion
		22 Binding of Isaac
		23 Burial of Sarah
		24 Marriage of Isaac
		25 Genealogy of Abraham 26 Death (175)

TABLE 1: Overview of Abra(ha)m's Biography

This type of biography is filled with secondary characters that are generally immediate kin to the hero. They supplement the portrait of the main subject by sharpening certain elements of his character. Opposition to the subject is temporary and hardly menacing. However, a major character in the Hebrew episode narrative is God who is invariably personally touched by the encounter with the hero. It is not surprising, therefore, that many of the anthropomorphic passages in the Old Testament tend to be found in these episodic narratives. Furthermore, because each scene is relatively self-contained, the passage of time is not stressed, and the setting remains purely ornamental. Paradoxically, perhaps, these conditions endow the complete portrait with timelessness, thus allowing episodes to belong to each and every period in which it is recalled.

The episodic biography possesses powerful attributes. Because it pares down individual acts into exemplary behavior, the episodic biography permits the audience to locate within it embodiments of the national character. Because it trades on paradigmatic behavior, the audience finds it possible to make constant connections between heroic action in the past and potential model behavior in the present. For example, it is impossible not to recognize that one of the early stories told about Abraham, in which God sends a plague against a pharaoh who would take Sarah into his harem, foreshadows Israel's experiencing slavery and freedom. In brief, then, the story of Abraham and his many adventures invites readers to duplicate the close rapport he has with God and thus to also be worthy of the goals he achieved.

2. The Melodramatic Biography: The Story of Jacob

The melodramatic biography is the second prominent way that the Hebrews depicted the life of an ancestor. Unlike what we have seen in the story of Abraham, this form of biography does not convey idealized behavior; rather, it explores the hero's inner world. A full portrait of the subject is not achieved by joining a series of integral attributes, but by pursuing the character of the hero, progressively and deliberately, over a span of time and space. Thus, by the end of any melodramatic biography, the hero acquires a personality that is unique and non-transferable. Let us use the story of Jacob as an example.

The melodramatic biography shows an interest in the early life and destiny of the hero. In the case of Jacob, it is presented through an oracle given to his mother (Genesis 25:23) and through scenes in which Jacob gains through trickery rights and privileges that were due his older brother. In the Jacob story, trickery becomes a thematic leitmotif that binds a number of narratives associated with him. (In the story of David, whose name means "beloved," sexual attraction is the equivalent theme.) Thus trickery, successfully negotiated but ultimately destructive, appears in the stories about people who are associated with Jacob, including his wives, Leah and Rachel, his father-in-law Laban, his sons, Simeon and Levi at Shechem (ch. 34), and his daughter-in-law Tamar (ch. 38). The most brilliant example occurs in the episodes that surround the story of Joseph and his brothers, episodes that are themselves embedded within the biography of Jacob.[17] The death scenes in melodramatic biographies tend to be highly developed, so that the will of the dying ancestor can impress itself on future generations. Such long-range plotting generates a diversity of perspectives and multiplies the levels of irony afforded by the individual's situation.

A major characteristic of melodramatic biographies is the tendency to divide the life of the ancestor into two major portions. In the case of Jacob, all of his biography is sandwiched within two scenes that feature dim-eyed patriarchs bestowing birthrights, blessings, and parting kisses to the younger of two brothers (at chapters 27 and 48). The first part of Jacob's life-story is framed by otherworldly encounters, respectively, at Bethel when Jacob has a vision of a ladder to heaven (28:10-22) and at the Jabbok river, where Jacob wrestles with a mysterious creature and acquires a new name (32:25-33). This portion is single-minded in its interest in Jacob's personal development and prosperity. Jacob survives all odds and succeeds in fulfilling the goals as established early in his life. [Table 2.]

---

[17]   On trickery as a motif in the Hebrew Bible, see Niditch 1987, especially the chapters (3 and 4) that deal with the Jacob stories.

Table 2 : Overview of Jacob's Biography
(Read as newspaper's columns)

Canaan (Beersheva, Bethel)		Paddan-Aram		Canaan (2)		Egypt	
Birth	25:19-26	At Laban: love struck	29:1-14	Struggle with divinity+etiology ("No longer Jacob, but Israel")	32:23-33	[Beersheva: Promise to return]	46:1-5
1. Tricking Esau: bekôrâ/firstborn	25:29-34	Jacob's marriage/Laban's trick	29:13-30	Esau (meeting/separation)	33:12-17	genealogy: Sons of Israel NB: 70 total	46:6-26
2. Tricking Isaac/Esau via Rebecca: bekôrâ/ blessing [NB brackets: Esau's marriages]	27:1-40	The sons of Jacob	29:31-30:21	Shechem (rape of Dinah) *Simon/Levi	34:1-31	1. Joseph gets Goshen 2. Jacob settles at Ramses [NB: complaint at 47:9]	47:1-5 47:6-12
Escape to Laban (Rebecca) sending to Laban (Isaac)	27:41-46 28:1-28	Jacob tricks toward wealth	30:31-25-43	Stele at Bethel "no more Jacob...[but] Israel"	35:1-15	Jacob: do not bury me here	47:27-31
Dream/ vow (Bethel)	28:10-22	Jacob's flight (theft of teraphim)	31:1-17	Benjamin+Rachel's death *Reuben & incest	35:16-20 36:21-22	Jacob (blind) adopts/blesses sons of Joseph (Ephraim, plus)	48:1-22
—>		Laban's chases Jacob Treaty with Laban	31:17-42 31:43-32:4	Genealogy: Jacob; death of Isaac Genealogy: Esau \ Edom	36:23-43	Testament of Jacob	49:1-28
		Readying to meet Esau	32:3-22	Joseph and his brothers (1)	37:2-36	Death of Jacob	49:29-33
		—>		Judah and Tamar	38:1-30	Exodus to bury Jacob	50:1-12
				Joseph slave in Egypt Joseph and his brothers (2) —>	39:1-40:45 40:46-45:28	Return to Egypt	50:14

The second part of Jacob's biography is framed by a seventeen-year span in which Joseph lived in the Promised Land and an equal period in which Jacob finished his life in Egypt. In this second section Jacob is but a presence, resignedly witnessing the fragmentation of his own hopes and aspirations. But, even as he loses his power to control his immediate destiny, he grows in omniscience and in his ability to shape the distant future. Essentially, in the second portion of the melodramatic biography, be it about Jacob, Saul, or David, the hero watches his children crush his hopes and aspirations, and they often do so by adopting the same instruments (trickery for Jacob; sexual drive for David) that worked so well for their father.

It is curious that in the best melodramatic biographies, those of Jacob and David, the Hebrew narrator found it plausible to repeat versions of essentially the same story. For example, in both biographies the hero acquires two sisters: Jacob from Laban (Genesis 29) and David from Saul (1 Samuel 18). Both tales describe the rape of daughters, leading to the rampages of brothers (Dinah in Genesis 34 and Tamar in 2 Samuel 13). Both tell about the appropriation of the hero's concubines (Reuben in Genesis 35 and Absalom in 2 Samuel 16), and both feature brother rising against brother (Joseph in Genesis 37 and Adonijah in 1 Kings 1-3).[18]

---

[18] See the articles of Greenstein 1990, Ho 1999, Auld 2000, and Wesselius 2001. Although they offer similarly conceived themes, these authors do not cite each other.

Largely because it is so tied to the achievements and the disappointments of an ancestor, the melodramatic biography lacks the versatility, transferability and adaptability of the episodic biography. Yet, melodrama is the stuff by which we measure the passion of the human spirit. Sharply edged and non-transferable, the portrait drawn in melodrama intrigues us not merely because of its antiquity or venerability, but because of the uncanny familiarity of the experiences it describes. If the episodic portrait of an Abraham, a Moses, and a Samson could give comfort to the Hebrews about the close connection between their ancestor and God, the melodramatic portraits of a Jacob and a David could teach them that human lives need not be perfect for God to invest them with meaning and purpose.

E. Looking Ahead

I end this first lecture with the hope that you may now better understand how Hebrew historiography relies on a set of conventions, how it generates highly theological themes, and how it constructs manifestly edifying paradigms. In so doing, it presents us with an optimized and didactic version of its past rather than one we can enter into our history books. Yet, there is good evidence that the Hebrew writers had access to traditions that were themselves based on historical reality and that they had consulted usable royal records. In the second lecture, we will revisit this material to see what it discloses about the history of ancient Israel.

A Response to Lecture One

Archie C. C. LEE

B. A., M. Div. (CUHK); Ph. D. (Edinburgh)
Professor, Department of Religion, The Chinese University of Hong Kong

Ancient West Asia and the Hebrew Bible
Archie C. C. LEE

Having this opportunity for me to respond to Professor Sasson's first lecture of the Chuen King Lecture not only is my honour, but also something I am very pleased to do.

The Bible is one of the precious religious writings of humanity. It has shaped many people's views on the universe and life; it has nurtured numerous people's religious consciousness and daily ethical living; and, at the same time, it stimulates social participation and spiritual practices in great many believers. How to study the Bible has been the first question of concern for communities of believers over the ages. "How to read" and "Why to read," as well as "Who to read" have close relationship. In the past, exegesis has undermined or rejected the role of reader participation in the reading process. In some traditional and conservative churches, the communities of believers thought that if the Bible was the Word revealed by God, it would have to be heard through the inspiration of the Holy Spirit in humble spiritual approach; all human thinking and effort would be useless. To have a real understanding of God's Word, according to this train of thought, we have to eliminate all human elements. The reader is only the humble listener and passive receiver. However, is there someone who can really strip off distinctions in culture, experience, sex, social status and semantics, to listen to God's Word outside the bounds of human writings and languages, and also be able to understand it and put it into practice? Who can disregard the existing models and directions of interpretation passed onto our communities and social groups where we belong? That churches of different denominations and traditions have their own ways of Bible study and pattern of thinking can be traced in general back to various ecclesiastical lines.

They only repeat the individual doctrines that they have inherited, making them absolute and divine. What the academics call the objective, historical-critical approach has been prevalent for a while, gaining control of the whole discipline of Biblical research. In fact that theory also has its principle of presupposition, presuming the value and objectivity of history; believing that, through criticism we could get to the truth of the matter, restore the scene of history. It denies the role of the reader, but, at the same time accepts some of the proposition and formulation of theologies or doctrines; for example, the concepts of assuming God acts in history and the framework of salvation-history (a position usually associating with G. von Rad[1]). Protestant scholars in particular used to think that the Prophets in the Bible represented the essence of the Hebrew tradition. The Torah was a latecomer that has perverted the Hebrew faith and brought defilement and rebellion to the tradition of the prophets and therefore corrupted the Word of God. Therefore, it has been considered that the Prophets must have been completed before the priests, and that means, the Pentateuch (the Torah) after the

---

[1] Gerhard von Rad, *The message of the prophets*, translated from the German by D. M. G. Stalker (London: SCM Press, 1965).

Prophets (a view expressed J. Wellhausen[2] in Preface to his monumental work on the Prolegomenon). The whole Hebrew Bible awaits completion with the redemptive incarnation of Jesus in the New Testament.

In the past twenty years, there have been enormous changes in the approach to Biblical research. Historical-critical method have received criticism from all sides. When such method of absolute superiority has been thrown away, there appeared the situation of multi-faceted developments: many views of minority or marginalized groups emerged; various ways and theories of reading championing gender, social strata, races, colours, regions flourished; the workers, aboriginals, women, Korean Minjung Bible reading, grass Indian Dalit criticism, the American black movement and interpretation theories of the Asians and Asian Americans, Latin Americans and Africans, etc. have enriched the contextual reading of the Bible and the sense and sensitively to the Scriptures; these different approaches have also strengthened the interaction and dialogues between the text and the reader.

One regrettable phenomenon is, the neglect of such biblical research methods on the Bible world; especially the ignorance of many readers about the contexts of the Bible, the world behind the text. They only put emphasis on the situation of the reader and the present form of the scriptures, but neglect the

---

[2]   Julius Wellhausen, *Prolegomena to the history of ancient Israel* (New York: Meridian Books, 1957).

backgrounds of the world of Ancient Near East (West Asia), which has discolourized and impoverished the interpretations.

Professor Sasson is a world-renowned Hebrew Bible scholar. He has inherited abundant and excellent Jewish traditions. On one hand he shows love and affection to the Biblical scriptures, and studies them rigorously; on the other hand he adopts an open attitude of interpretation. To those scriptures not so easy to understand, he accepts debates on reasonable grounds, admitting that these are uncertainties in meaning and ambiguities. Professor Sasson is one of the few Jewish biblical scholars in American Christian seminaries. He can make use of the Hebrew story-telling tradition in the Old Testament, to demonstrate clearly and vividly how story-telling can be an art form, by means of images and sounds of the words, the use of grammar, characteristics of the sentence structure, to express the writing motive of the author and the theme of the story. Hebrew stories use same materials of the culture of the ancient west Asia, customs and practices of their daily life and models of literature, to show its teachings and central ideas. The World of the Ancient Near East (Ancient West Asia) is much bigger than the Biblical world. It is an enormous sky that has nurtured the Bible; its long history and great civilization have bewildered us so much. Professor Sasson has pointed out an important truth: the birth of the Bible means the end of the civilization of the West Asia. Fortunately the Renaissance in Europe and the Enlightenment movement have started the quest for the ancient world civilization, which has resurrected the world of the ancient West Asia, as if West Asia, through Biblical research, can be recovered.

Having had long periods of hard work, scholars have made tremendous contributions in the interpretation of ancient writings and restoration of the archaeological artifacts. Today we can say with certainty that, the Ancient West Asian religion has established an important milestone in human civilizations. It helps us to understand the context of the Bible, how God's people grew in the environment of West Asian culture, assimilated the local culture and, at the same time, with their own religious experience, had created a profound religion of revelation. The religious world that they have witnessed, rightly demonstrates the miraculous divine, the mystery of life and the dynamic tension between God and humanity. The revelatory religion of the Pentateuch and the prophets show that the transcendence of life cannot be reached and grasped by human being; but the Wisdom Books never forsakes life, keeps on exploring and searching, confirming the predicament and possibility of human's innate transcendence.

Professor Sasson's lecture clearly shows the importance of Ancient West Asian research on the Hebrew Bible. The Scriptures are texts not without context. This text has its own world, and its world contains factors of a concrete community, geography, culture, environment, history, politics and economy. The Hebrew story-telling tradition that Professor Sasson here emphasizes contains mainly two kinds of narrative forms: episodes and melodramas. In the episode, the stories appear in short narratives, like the main themes in an opera. Between episodes there may not be any connection. In the melodrama, there are various acts joining in a series. The personalities of the heroic characters and their expressions are revealed in the text. These two forms of stories all inherited from the literature and religion of Ancient West Asia, from oral tradition or literary creation in written form, they were collected and redacted in an integrated manner as we have them in the Biblical text. They manifest characteristics of pluralistic, multi-dimensional, repetitive, as well as contradictory as in West Asian literature. Many scholars have tried to reconstruct and understand them but still cannot fully comprehend. In the text, the stories have multi-meanings; from aetiology to ethical teachings. The story of the Tower of Babel and the sacrifice of Isaac by Abraham have clearly expressed the many levels of meanings in the text. Just as what Professor Sasson has said, these stories, especially about heroes of the past, were used as a model in the Bible, which have also become models of right behavior for today's readers.

As religious documents, the Bible has the functions to educate, nurture and to inspire spirituality and religiosity. Its contents, though having a strong sense of Hebrew nationalism, also have the meaning of transcending the boundaries of races and nations. Professor Sasson does not go further to explain how this ancient Hebrew religious document relates to today's Asian and Chinese Christians. If we understand the origin of the scriptures, that many resources and documents from West Asian culture and religions have been adopted and made use of in the construction and articulation of the faith of Israel, then we will come to appreciate the importance of investigating into the world of West Asia on one hand; and, on the other hand, in our own comprehension and practice, we can understand that our Asian context and cultural religious resources too have certain important roles to play. Our world will be enriched through the extension of time and space. From West Asia to East Asia; from ancient to modern, the integration between our imaginary world and the textual world not only helps us to comprehend the world of the scriptures but also integrate the past and the present, Chinese and the non-Chinese, which enables the interaction and inter-relatedness of human explorations and struggles in different communities and various regions at different times.

Professor Sasson, through the insightful grasp of the characteristics of Hebrew literature, explains some misunderstandings of the scriptures: translation and interpretation problems arising out of the inappropriate suffix of consonants after the vowel text. Therefore, it is imperative that in our reading of the scriptures we have to first of all do a critical assessment of the received text and various ancient translation and manuscripts in order to arrive at a text, which is presumably close to the original form. Besides, as the Hebrew words or phrases are either of male or female genders with no neutral gender, Professor Sasson has pointed out that the word "God" has been understood as in male form. There is no indication that YHWH is a male God. On the surface this explanation seems to be quite acceptable. However, the use of a male gender has produced undesirable effect, which was not the author's intention, in the long process; the believers of the church have unconsciously accepted and imparted a gender biased attitude and mindset. Furthermore, in comprehending Genesis 2 and 3, the church has placed the reasons of the fall of humanity and the original sin onto the incident of Eve giving the forbidden fruit for Adam to eat. Hence, women have inherited tremendous discrimination; sex and desires have been excluded from the life of the believers and marginalized in Christian teachings. If, true as what Professor Sasson has said, the pronoun "he" being used for God has no sexual denotations and gender implications, then, is it also acceptable to use "she"? It seems natural to take God as father, but why to take God as mother will create great reactions in church and many believers feel offended?

In theological thinking and use of semantics in Chinese Christian writings in Late Ming and Early Qing China, God was often referred to as "Great Parents in Heaven" (大父母) . A Chinese Christian by the name of Han Lin (韓霖) from Shanxi wrote "The Book of Admonition" (鐸書) which intended to impart ethical teaching at the local village level. He integrated Biblical teaching and Chinese folk religious concepts in his writing. He used the Chinese tradition, "Giving birth" to describe the creation of God: God "giving birth to heaven, earth, gods, men, things." God is our Great Parents (Father and Mother). This concept of God as Parents is more appropriate than God as Father. In Chinese, the honorific pronoun " 祂 " may also be used to replace the gender exclusive ones, "he" or "she." Perhaps this tiny technical consideration may in an unexpected way address the inadequacies of the Hebrew and English language (and other western languages).

SECOND LECTURE

On Hebrew History

SECOND LECTURE
ON HEBREW HISTORY

A. THE PROBLEM
1. The Sweep of Biblical Historiography

In the previous lecture, I focused on the way Hebrews wrote about their past. I discussed how they worked through a set of conventions, developed themes that were theological in motivation, and presented their history through a series of artistically drawn lives of ancestors and kings. The Bible, then, presents an optimized and didactic version of the past that, while it continues to astonish us for its spiritual and literary sensitivity, severely limits our capacity to rely on it in writing the real history of Israel. Let us briefly look first at the Hebrew version of Israel's history.

In the first four books of the Bible, Genesis through Numbers, the Hebrew narrator tells us that God chooses Abraham and directs him to Canaan, a promised land. Episodes in the life of Abraham reveal how he takes control of significant segments of that land through military victory (Genesis 14:1-16), covenants (Genesis 14: 17-24; 21:22-34), and purchases (Genesis 23). Control is maintained by the Isaac but, despite the patriarchs' exceptional life, it is lost when Jacob moves his family to Egypt, inaugurating a slavery that lasts 430 years (Exodus 12:40). This telling is frequently moving and, by telling us about opportunities lost, sets us up for the story of the promise regained.

Moses leads the Hebrews out of Egypt and the story slows down during a forty-year wanderings while Israel, never quite appreciating God's great miracles in its behalf, receives all the laws it will need. From this moment, the narrative acquires its own characteristic as it winds through the books of Joshua, Judges, Samuel, and Kings, earning the label the "Deuteronomistic History." It is important to note that from the Hebrews' perspective Joshua, led Israel to *re*conquer the land once held by the patriarchs. The re-conquest is presented as a *Blitzkrieg*, successful only after the Hebrews learn to trust God's directions in dealing with the city-states then in power. Nonetheless, the program that unfolds gives hint of a progressive distancing from God. Thus, the Hebrews take Jericho without problem after consulting God; but they experience defeat at Ai when they initially fail to consult God and they lose the possibility of controlling Gibeon because they do not consult God. The Book of Judges repeatedly replays this oscillation between faith with its resultant success and apostasy with its consequent punishment.

But the Hebrews, feeling unequal to their neighbors, prefer having a human king rather than the kingship of God. In the Book of Samuel is recorded a debate about the virtues and vices of kingship as a prelude to the selection of Saul. With David kingship is institutionalized and with Solomon it acquires oriental trappings. The rest of the story deals with the split of the monarchy into the kingdoms of Israel and of Judah. Israel almost constantly sins against God, and succumbs to the Assyrians in 721. Judah, occasionally led by a fervent believer (such as Hezekiah and Josiah), survives until its sins bring the Babylonians to sack Jerusalem and to take its leaders into Exile. It takes many years for the temple to be rebuilt and even longer for the descendants of the exiles, in a second Exodus, to return home. In the Hebrew Bible, the story ends as God is giving his people one more chance for the promised land.

2. The Dearth of Independent Testimony for Hebrew History

So much for the story as told by narrators for whom God is the only true and constant protagonist. It is a story so wonderful that we retell it almost verbatim in our history books and even make movies out of good portions of it. Yet, as historians we have a problem with it. The narrator is not interested in economic, military, or political causes for fortunes, good and bad; rather, the quality of the relationship his people have with God is made to control the destiny of Israel. Because historians cannot rely on historical testimony in which a deity is a major player and cannot explain historical events by assigning them to divine causes, historians must posit more mundane explanations.

Ever since the early nineteenth century, historians have insisted that at least two witnesses of an event are needed before a critical analysis can be launched about its authenticity or usefulness. Yet, a good portion of what is told to us in the Bible as the history of the Hebrew people has as yet to be corroborated by independent evidence. Most of us take it for granted that we shall not likely find useful evidence of Adam and Eve, of Cain and Abel, of Noah and the Flood. But we are still looking for evidence of the existence, in person or in equivalent, to such vividly recreated personalities as Abraham and Sarah, Jacob and Rachel, Joseph and the Pharaoh who sponsored him, Moses and the Pharaoh who opposed him, Saul, David, and Solomon. All these figures played major roles in Israel's telling of its story, but they have so far left us no trace of their presence. Ironically, only when the Assyrians and Babylonians impose their authority on Israel and Judah do we meet with extra-biblical reference to such kings as Omri, Ahab and Jehu, Hezeqiah and Jehoiaqim. It does not get any easier in the Persian period, because we have as yet to find confirmation of Ezra, Nehemiah, or any of the leaders credited with bringing the Hebrews back to their homeland.

3. The Credibility of Hebrew Dating[19]

To complicate matters even more, we lack a basis by which to assess the biblical chronology in order to place events displayed in the Bible on a realistic historical chart. This is especially true for the period before the Kingdoms of Israel and Judah. Hebrew historiographers depended on two very eccentric methods, themselves not very compatible, to graph the passage of time: chronography and genealogy.

CHRONOGRAPHY. The Hebrews could place in a sequence the ages at which ancestors gave birth to their sons and in this way measure intervals between sequences of births. Yet the numbers they give us are unrealistic even after the Flood. Abraham is 100 and Jacob is in his 70s when they sire their first children, and these numbers differ when found in the Hebrew, Greek versions, and Samaritan version of the Bible. Many of these numbers are transparently didactic, replaying favored numbers,

---

[19] A recent volume on the issue is Hughes 1990. Good discussions and overviews in Cryer 1987 and Cogan 1992.

such as three, seven, and forty. Moreover, the entire chronological scheme of the Hebrew Bible seems to have been reshaped much later when 4000 years were made to separate Creation from the rededication of the temple in the Maccabean period, just a couple centuries before Christ.[20]

GENEALOGY. The other method of Hebrew historiography was just as eccentric. The Hebrews differentiated between blocs of time by the passage of generations. Ten generations separated creation from the flood and ten generations distanced the flood from the election of Abraham. Major figures, often the subject of narratives, were placed in the seventh slot of a genealogical list or its multiples (for example Enoch in Genesis 5:21, Eber in 11: 16, Boaz in Ruth 4:21). It is well known, for example, that the genealogy of Jesus was crafted to be forty-two generations deep, in three subdivisions, each of fourteen (that is twice seven) generations.[21]

In most cases, the two systems, chronography and genealogy, clashed; yet they were retained just the same because they conveyed different forms of truth. For example, the Hebrews are said to be in Egypt for 430 years, yet genealogically only four, at most five, generations separate Jacob from Moses.

---

[20] Very helpful tables are given in De Vries 1962.
[21] A succinct overview is by Wilson 1992. For the operation of this convention, see Sasson 1978. Notice how the numbers of years and of generations can differ in the Septuagint (Greek) and Samaritan versions of Scripture from what we have in the Hebrew Bible.

B. THE TOOLS FOR A SOLUTION

1. Internal Inspection

Biblical scholars compensate for this dearth of information and the eccentricity of Hebrew chronology in a number of ways. There was a time when we isolated diverse independent documents within Scripture, the best-known being labeled J, E, D, and P, and tried to gain historical control by studying them comparatively. This method, labeled the *Documentary Hypothesis*, has proven invaluable for discussing the origin and growth of Hebrew tradition, but it has not succeeded in authenticating Biblical history. (See First and Third Lectures.)

2. Circumstantial Evidence

Scholars then tried to find circumstantial proof for the Bible's version of history by finding a place for them in their neighbor's history. For example, the Hyksos period in Egypt from around 1650 BC was regarded as a plausible setting for Joseph and so also as backdrop for the Exodus; documents from the reign of Hammurabi of Babylon, around 1750 BCE, were used to situate Abraham as he battled Amraphel of Shinar, allegedly Hammurabi himself. But this approach has not proved persuasive because it depended on circular reasoning.[22]

----

[22] Today, one comes across attempts to synchronize personalities from Israel's early history with rulers from the 2nd millennium BCE mostly in the literature of "conservative" scholars. An exception is the appeal of the Amarna age as a background to Moses and the Exodus, on which see the Third Lecture. Recent discussions about the power of Elam during the early second millennium BCE has renewed occasional interest in postulating an Elamite incursion into Canaan. The notions have not yet jelled into a plausible focus for discussion.

3. Paralleling through Recovered Archives

For a good portion of the twentieth century, however, scholarship devoted an incredible amount of energy and focus to reaffirm the historicity of Israel. Especially in its early phases, it established analogies between social activities reported in the Bible with ancient Near Eastern documents that have specific dates. In America, where the Bible is a cultural icon and the locus of emotional investment, William Albright and his disciples were especially keen to establish the historical trustworthiness of the Patriarchal and Exodus histories. In Europe, where the Bible is above all a seed for its most profound literature, much more attention was devoted to analyzing the accuracy of Monarchic Israel.[23] I want to give you a brief report on this effort, since we will come back to it in the third and final Chuen King lecture.

TELL EL-AMARNA. In the late nineteenth century, a hoard of tablets written in locally influenced Akkadian proved to have come from Tell el-Amarna, the site of Akhetaten. For a relatively brief time in the 14th century BC, Akhetaten was the capital of the Egyptian Empire under Ikhnaten, allegedly the first monotheistic king in history. The information these tablets carried created a sensation, not least because among the people mentioned in them were the Hapirus, presented as a population that was shifty in behavior as well as in allegiance. Very promptly, the Hapirus were

---

[23] An enormous literature has developed around these matters. Two classic works that sought to set the early periods of Israel firmly in history are de Vaux 1978 and Speiser's commentary to Genesis (1964). Two works that began dismantling the historicizing structure are Thompson 1974 and van Seters 1975. The material is reviewed in all recent biblical dictionaries, under such entries as "Historiography," "Patriarchal Age," or "Israel, History,"

linked with the ʿibrî, the Hebrews and much ink was spilled on the origins of Israel among them. Since then, we have learned that the Hapirus were broadly scattered in time and place during the second millennium, that they were transient people, divorced from their own communities, and that anyone deemed treacherous was called by that name. So not at all equivalent to how Israel portrayed itself. Still, there is enough in the dossier of the Hapirus to keep serious scholars intrigued by their connection to the Hebrews, especially because the Hapirus disappear from records when Israel was jelling as a nation.[24]

MARI. Right after the First World War, a series of great archival discoveries were made in the Levant, in Ugarit, Nuzi, Mari, and, much more recently, at Ebla. Each of these sites delivered large caches of texts that stem from a comparatively narrow time period. The Mari archives come to us from the Middle Euphrates valley of the eighteenth century BCE. They give us much information about the Amorites, West Semitic people that, according to many scholars, were of the same stock as the future Hebrews.[25] I will speak more about them in a moment.

NUZI. The archives from Nuzi a village near Kirkuk in Iraq were recovered in the 1930s. They yielded much information about the social life of the Hurrians, a major ethnic group. The material

---

[24] The most recent monograph on the topic is Loretz 1984. Overviews (with specific points of view) are in Lemche 1992 and Astour 1999.

[25] Several essays by Malamat (1989, 1999) discuss connections between Mari and the biblical world. Two fine overviews are Margueron 1992 (archaeology) and Durand 1992 (epigraphy). See also Sasson 1998 and Fleming 1998. Volumes 92 (1998) and 93 (1999) of the *Revue d'Assyriologie* include a number of articles on the links between Amorites and Hebrews.

comes from the early in the fourteenth century. It includes many contracts dealing with purchase, lease, marriage, adoption, and exchange, as well as agreements that brought men and women into brotherly and sisterly connections. The Nuzi documents were quickly mined for comparison with the behavior of the patriarchs of Israel. Scholars searched for the presence of patriarchy, adoption of next of kin, deathbed blessing, marriages to sisters, and the like, hoping to find comparisons that would establish a date for when the patriarchs were active. This approach was strongly adopted in the years after the Second World War, especially in America. It lost much of its persuasive power, however, when it was shown that the social settings were not unique to the second millennium BCE and that the interpretation of the evidence was often too skewed to match the Bible's.[26]

UGARIT. Also in the 1930s, excavations at Ugarit, a port city just north of Latakia in Syria, produced an archive from the 14th and 13th century. Unlike Nuzi, Ugarit was the Hong Kong of its days, a cosmopolitan, business-oriented, city with many resident foreign traders. We do not hear of any Hebrews among Ugarit's residents; but from the documents that were written in a unique alphabetic cuneiform, we learn a lot about the religion of Canaan, which up until then was known to us almost exclusively from the antagonistic testimony of the Bible. We are discovering from them that, except for their worship of many gods rather than one, the

---

[26] Fine overviews on Nuzi are in Maidman 1995 (severely critical of comparing Nuzi and biblical experiences) and Morrison 1992 (willing to discuss them). The works of Thompson and van Seters cited in note 5 above include elaborate discussions.

Canaanites and the Hebrews were images of each other.[27]

EBLA and EMAR. Other archives continue to be found in recent decades, and they too have been placed at the service of reconstructing the Hebrew past. When documents dating to the twenty-fourth century BCE, so practically from the dawn of history, were discovered at Ebla (modern Tell Mardikh) near Aleppo in Syria, they were first misread because they were written in an unfamiliar script. A few Biblical scholars used these badly read texts to link the patriarchs of Israel to the Ebla context. But the Ebla culture was fully urbanized, not at all like the tribal world the Bible describes. [28] The finds from Emar, at the bend of the Euphrates (Tell Meskene) and almost contemporaneous with Ugarit, are still being assessed for their contents that could be enlighten us about the Hebraic world, especially its society (Fleming 1995).

4. Unearthing the Bible

In contrast to the rich harvest of documents recovered from such sites as those mentioned above, relatively few texts were recovered from the land of the Hebrews. A few stone monuments have been found, mentioning names of kings found in the Bible.[29] For example, the Mesha and Tel Dan stelas mention the dynasties of Omri and of

---

[27]   A good overview of Ugarit, its history and culture is in van Soldt 1995. More detailed are the encyclopedic articles of Yon 1992 (on archaeology) and of Pardee & Bordreuil 1992. The recent book of M. Smith (2001) is undisciplined, but will repay close reading.

[28]   Ebla studies are now almost free of the wild speculations about its role as shaper of Hebrew history and culture that marred the scholarly literature immediately after the discovery of its archives; see Milano (1995) and Biggs (1992) for accessible summaries of information, the latter with a corrective on early excesses.

[29]   A nice collection of extra-biblical texts relevant to ancient Israel is found in Smelik 1991 and in Hallo and Younger 2000: 137-238 (diverse authors).

David.[30] We have a couple of inscriptions, notably one carved in a water channel in Siloam, possibly dated to Hezeqiah.[31] There is a striking text painted on plaster at Deir Alla in Jordan that mentions the non-Hebrew prophet Balaam son of Beor. Ironically, Balaam is not only the only prophet recorded in the Bible to be cited in non-biblical sources, but also one of the few personalities set in pre-monarchic times to be so mentioned.[32] We also have quite a few ostraca, texts written on pottery fragments, from the Divided Monarchy that were found in Samaria, Lachish, and Arad, telling us of the hardship experienced during foreign invasions. We are finding ostraca in Transjordan and clay impressions of seals that were once stamped on letters written on papyrus and leather. Among these impressions we are finding the names of so many people mentioned in the Bible as living during the last days of the Kingdom of Judah, that scholars wonder whether they are being fabricated in some basement in Israel or Jordan. All this material is welcome, of course; but it does not contribute significantly to establishing a history of Israel independent from the Bible.[33]

---

[30] The Mesha stela is widely quoted, for example in Pritchard 1969: 320-321. A readable study (with nice bibliography) is Smelik 1991: 29-50, 171-172; but see also his 1992. The Tel Dan inscription has received spectacular coverage because it mentions "The House of David." After much conflicting opinions, it is now favored that the phrase refers to the dynasty of David rather than to the Kingdom of Judah; good discussions are in Demsky 1996, Lemaire 1998, and Na'aman 2000. For a possible mention of the same phrase in the slightly older (mid-9th c.) Mesha stela, see Lemaire 1994.

[31] There has been much discussion recently whether or not the Siloam inscription in Hellenistic rather than from monarchic Judah. Most responsible scholarship retains its dating to the times of Hezeqiah; see Norin 1998 for the latest discussion.

[32] The inscription (actually a number of inscriptions on a plaster wall, some in bad state of preservation) has received much attention. A good monograph is Hackett 1984; but see also the accessible overviews in Hackett 1986 and Barré 1997.

[33] The bibliography on this material has swelled dangerously in the past decades. Some famous examples (from Samaria, etc.) are treated in Smelik 1992. Lemaire 1992a provides easy access to encyclopedic articles on ostraca collections found at diverse sites.

In recent years, analytic methods used in the archeology of Israel have become increasingly sophisticated. High-tech tools are now being employed to establish the dating of levels, to analyze bone, seed, and soil samples, and to assemble a new set of circumstantial evidence that could test Biblical testimony without ignoring the dearth of written documents so far recovered. In the minutes I have left, I want to give a brief review of where we are regarding the formation of Israel. Do keep in mind, however, that in Biblical studies suggestions are many and gain acceptance for short durations only.

C. DEBATES and SPECULATIONS
1. Primeval History

In the first eleven chapters of Genesis, the Hebrew describes the world that preceded the election of Abraham. Because historical research cannot validate any biblical statement on the early history of the world, most prudent scholars skip deciding on the historicity of Adam and Eve, Cain and Able, Methuselah, or Enoch. Yet, if you surf the internet, you will read articles by scientists and academics that present the Flood and its historicity in scientific detail. Recent expositions describe cataclysmic floods that are said to have occurred in the Arabian Desert around 20, 000 years ago or on the shores of the Black Sea some 7,500 years ago.[34] That such events occurred is possible, of course; but it is not credible to believe that they would have inspired Flood traditions recorded millennia later in Mesopotamia and Hebrew

---

[34] The flood of 20,000 years ago (plus or minus) is said to have occurred in the Arabian Peninsula, see Teller (et al., 2000). The Back Sea flooding of 7,600 years ago continues to be discussed in the literature and in the media; for now see Ryan and Pitman 1999.

texts, if only because flood narratives are found internationally and are told across many centuries. Additionally, such suggestions also do not appreciate how Flood narratives are used in particular cultures. For instance, the Biblical example is not there just to satisfy curiosity about world calamities, but to explain why God, finding no improvement in the moral values of humans even after his Flood, nevertheless gave them a new opportunity. And he did so, not by blanketing the world with another flood, but by selecting an Abraham through whom to advance higher standards for decency and justice.[35]

2. The Patriarchal Age

The debate about the historicity of the patriarchal age has been protracted and tough. As stated above, the case for the historical reliability of the Genesis material on Abraham, Isaac, and Jacob, has been largely circumstantial, with no extra-biblical documentation to support what the Bible says. Yet, there is reason to keep the issue open.[36] For example, the Mari archives of the 18th century BCE (cited above) do offer us a vast literature on the relationship between settled cities and nomads. It is significant that leaders of tribal stock ruled the cities mentioned in the Mari texts while the leaders of tribes themselves displayed very urbanized tastes, very much reminiscent of Jacob's world when he reentered Canaan. The Mari records provide extensive information on tribal affiliation with places such as Harran in which the Hebrews placed their ancestors.

---

[35] See Sasson 1980.
[36] see Hendel 1997.

As it happens, we have information from the early second millennium about the existence of one tribe that plays a crucial role in Hebrew history, a tribe that provided Israel its first king. That tribe is the Binu-Yamina, a name that means "Southerners." The Mari documents contain much information about this tribe, which is revealed to be of Amorite, that is, of West Semitic stock. It consisted of five sub-tribes (not always in total harmony with each other), each of which was ruled by a leader who had dealings with powerful kingdoms. We can follow the story of one sub-tribe, the Rabbaeans, well into Roman times and we might be able to do the same with another, the Yarikhu, a sub-tribe whose name is based on that of the West-Semitic Moon god.

We recall that among the many towns assigned to the Hebrew tribe of Benjamin, also meaning "Southerners," is the famous city of Jericho, after God destroyed its walls. Now the name Jericho likely means "(dedicated to) the Moon (god)." Because there is no tradition of Moon worship in the region, it is tempting to suggest that the Yarikhu sub-tribe known from the Mari documents renamed Jericho after themselves, once they settled in the region. If so, the tribe of Benjamin would be unique so far among all of the Hebrew tribes to have had an antiquity that can be authenticated extra-biblically.[37]

---

[37] The hypothesis was made in Astour 1959, but has been largely neglected. Recently, Fleming (1998) has proposed something almost similar. On the Rabbaean tribes, see Astour 1978.

This is about as far as we can go in establishing historical reality for the patriarchal narratives, and it is not much at that. But the Mari records allow for other types of linkage. For example, we notice that two-thirds of personal names embedded in the patriarchal narratives do not occur elsewhere in the Bible; but they are cast in forms that were current among the Amorites of Mari.[38] The Mari archives also give us a wonderful entry into the world of story-telling such as was practiced in Israel, and rarely elsewhere. The letters exchanged among kings and courtiers could be very long, incredibly garrulous, with writers paying much attention to dialogue, embedding anecdotes, and adopting omniscience, not unlike the story-telling techniques found in Israel that I described in the previous lecture. A series of letters that report on how an envoy negotiated for his king a marriage with a princess reads very much like the story about Isaac acquiring a bride. Another dossier of letters detailing how a Mari King purchased land far from his own city-state reminds of territorial purchases Abraham and David made in Hebron (Genesis 23) and Jerusalem (2 Samuel 24). Maybe story-telling was also part of the heritage from the ancestral homeland.[39]

3. The Exodus

What the Bible tells us about the entry into Egypt is not implausible. Joseph is said to have gained a major position under pharaoh and seduced his father's tribe to settle in an Egyptian land, Goshen. Josephus, writing centuries later, attached Joseph to the Hyksos, Asiatic folks who came to rule Egypt in the 17th and 16th centuries

---

[38]   See the collection of elements in Zadok 1993.
[39]   See my remarks in Sasson 1998:108-111.

BCE, and the temptation for modern scholars has been to stay with the theory. From the Egyptian records, however, we know that from time immemorial people from Western Asia moved in and out of Egypt, some as artisans, some to purchase food, and to work in pharaoh's armies. We also know that individuals of Semitic stock rose in the pharaoh's administration, one of them, named Bay(a), becoming chancellor early in twelfth century.[40] So it is not necessary to link Joseph with the Hyksos period (17th century BCE), as it could have happened at any of a great number of periods of Egypt's history. But the sojourn of Israel in Egypt has been complicated not just by linkage with the Hyksos, but also by a desire to place Moses in the court of Pharaoh Akhnaten, because of their alleged common monotheistic ardor.[41] What defeats us here, ironically enough, is the wealth of detail that we have from the records of Egypt and Canaan. While they permit rather detailed historical reconstructions of both cultures during the Late Bronze Age, they cannot be tweaked into making room either for the exit of Israel from Egypt or for its entry into Canaan. Among the elements that are constantly sifted are: the mention of a people who may (or may not) be Israel in a monument by Pharaoh Merneptah datable to around 1210 BCE ; the well-documented havoc created late in the 13th century BCE by the Sea People (among whom were the Philistines) as they arrived from regions still not yet satisfactorily pinpointed; and the route taken by the Hebrews when many stops they are recorded making seem not to have existed in the late Bronze Age.[42]

---

[40]   There are theories that Bay(a) was a prototype for Moses.
[41]   See the third lecture.
[42]   The literature on the Exodus is immense; but luckily also highly repetitive. For a succinct report that supports its historicity, see Kitchen 1992; for one that does not, see Finkelstein and Silberman 2001: 48-71. See also Frerichs and Lesko 1997, who assemble the evidence from the Egyptian side.

We must also face the fact that we have not one trace of Israel's presence in Egypt. It is true that Egyptians would have shied away from recording the escape of such a large slave contingent from its control. Because slavery was known to Egypt, especially after the New Kingdom conquered in Western Asia, it is remarkable that we hear nothing about an enslavement of such a large group over so many centuries.[43] Many scholars, therefore, claim that the Exodus plays on a literary pattern that was repeatedly displayed in Hebrew lore, one in which God places his people at risk only to rescue them. We have already seen in the previous lecture that the story of Abram and Sarai in Egypt (Genesis 12) foreshadows the Exodus while the Restoration from the Babylonian exile reconfirm it. Still, when all is said and done, there is no reason why some movement out of Egypt, by some modest groups later associated with Israel, could not have taken place. However, once we shrink the proportions of the Exodus, we lose sight of what the Hebrews wanted most to convey through that story: That by force of his arm, God brought back his beloved Hebrews to the Promised Land.

4. The Conquest

As to the Conquest, the debate begins with the stela of Pharaoh Merneptah, possibly placing an entity called Israel in Canaan by around 1210 BCE. Yet, our detailed knowledge of the region at around 1200 BCE precludes the presence of any army of the size and caliber reported in the book of Joshua before the 11th century. Moreover, archaeology does not support the biblical version of a

---

[43] On slavery in Egypt, see Allam 2000.

unified campaign that destroyed such towns as Jericho and Ai, at least because these towns simply were not there to be destroyed. When they began to be settled, late in the twelfth century, they were more like villages than walled cities. There is currently a debate on whether the new settlements and homesteads that litter the central hilly region towards the end of the 2nd millennium (generally regarded as equivalent to the Judges period) conform to, or differ from, the Canaanite patterns of the preceding eras.

At any rate, most scholars have abandoned the notion of an armed conquest as described in Joshua. But the alternatives that are discussed today also present difficulties. One of the proposals depends on the book of Judges to suggest that the Hebrews infiltrated Canaanite settlements, over a long period of time and with many difficulties. Eventually, the Hebrews became farmers as they took arable land from their neighbors. Archaeology cannot confirm such a theory because it is difficult to distinguish between Hebrews and Canaanites just by their farming behavior. Moreover, the book of Judges seems most interested in explaining why, despite the successes of Joshua's armies, so much of the allegedly conquered territory remained in Canaanite hands. God kept them there, the book claims, to test the devotion of Israel.

The third, and in some ways most eccentric, vision of the conquest holds that Hebrews never came to the Promised Land. They were there all along, because they were Canaanites, like everyone else. One day, fed up by the machinations of corrupt officials and tyrannical rulers, rebellious Canaanites chose Yahweh as a just god and rid themselves of their tormentors. The thesis is interesting, but it rests on pure conjectures.[44] Yet, when shorn of its didactic (not to say moralistic) elements, we could be left with a potentially useful theory. We know that around 1170, Egyptian power in the region retreated, ceding land to invading people later associated with the Philistines. Because these upheavals destroyed trade and compromised the capacity to produce enough food, many Canaanites moved to the Judean highland, to care for smaller farms and to keep modest flocks. Life in the highlands was precarious, but because the region was not especially desirable, it could shelter these Canaanite from Philistine attacks. This could be a plausible scenario for the birth of Israel; but what role God played in it will be left to the next lecture.

5. The Monarchy

I must not end without alerting you to an emerging debate that is bound to be very heated. This debate focuses on the nature of the monarchies that ruled Israel and Judah after the split of Solomon's kingdom and before their destruction, respectively by the Assyrians and the Babylonians. Until recently, very few scholars doubted the existence of the first kings of Israel, Saul, David, and Solomon, even though no extra-biblical confirmation of their rule had surfaced. More commonly, scholars affirmed their existence, while at the same time expressing doubts that the colorful stories told about them in the books of Samuel and Kings have survived unembellished. The discovery at Tel Dan of a monuments that

---

[44] Succinct accounting of these issues can be found in most reference sets, under "Conquest" or "Occupation of Canaan." A fine overview is Miller 1977.

mentions the "House of David" has not particularly swayed scholars one way or another about David's deed, let alone his existence (see above).

Here is where archaeology has brought in new considerations, although to be candid about it, there is much debate.[45] Material remains have shown that Judah and Israel differed radically from each other. Israel, in the north, occupied a much larger space, had more fortified areas, produced many examples of monumental architecture, and involved itself in broader trade than Judah ever did. Even by reading the book of Kings, with its bias against the Northern Kingdom which it judged illegitimate, it is clear that the kings of Israel operated much more like the powerful Aramaean states to the north and that they played a very influential role in regional and even international politics. Because they lived at the center of power, dynasties in Israel behaved like those of the neighbors. Assassination and usurpation were common hazards. Their own stories about the creation of their kingdom have been lost to us; but it is possible that they included what is preserved now in the book Judges (chapters 7-9) about Judge Gideon and his son King Abimelech, two leaders from the tribes of Manasseh and Ephraim, core segments of the kingdom of Israel.

---

[45] I am relying here most on Finkelstein 1999 and on Finkelstein & Silberman 2000: 149-295. Reaction to the thesis has come from both archaeologists and historians, some criticizing its positions on merits, but others lamenting it for its potential to undermine the Bible's credibility as a source of history. Among its most severe critics is William Dever, lastly in 2001 and Anson Rainey, lastly in 2001a. A nice review of the debate about the debates is in Zevit 2002 (accessible on the internet <http://www.bsw.org/?l=71831&a=Comm01.html>).

Contrast this with Judah, a kingdom that was relatively stable and relatively isolated. For the entire duration of Israel's existence, Judah was its vassal. There is not much archeological evidence of a powerful state that can be linked to the time of David and Solomon. If anything, David and Solomon may have ruled a very provincial region, and the dynasty that David founded could not have hoped for anything more than modest achievement. More impressive is the archeological evidence that Judah began to display a state with a functioning administration only in the ninth century, so almost a century after its sister nation to the north. So I offer the following speculation:

As long as Israel was an active state, Judah remained in its shadow. But when Assyria destroyed the kingdom of Israel around 720, an enormous mass of refugees streamed south, bringing expertise in trade and administration to Jerusalem. Almost overnight Judah became a much more imposing state, and its historians began to craft a past worthy of its new status as the heir to all those who believed in the Hebrew God. Its theologians and its keepers of traditions imagined that David and Solomon once ruled an empire that included both Judah and Israel. Because of the sins of Solomon and the stupidity of his son Rehoboam, ten tribes broke away and created an independent throne in the north, the Kingdom of Israel. But the kings of Israel were largely hostile to the god of their ancestor. That god, Yahweh, brought the kingdom to an end, giving the kings of Judah the opportunity to recreate the empire of David, the beloved king. It is tempting to hypothesize that the biblical story of how the monarchy was established in Israel and Judah may in fact have created a retrograde image of reality.

D. LOOKING AHEAD

You have sat patiently though this lengthy litany of places, names and dates and you may be wondering what it all leads to, this detailing of how little we actually know or can confirm about Israel's origins or real history. In fact, this condition is quite the reverse from what obtained half a century ago, when in many quarters the Bible was read as history, especially beginning with the age of the patriarchs. Just after the 1960's, however, and especially after the war in Viet-Nam revealed how history can be manipulated for sinister purposes, a shift occurred from all studies that relied on historical methods to those that exploited literary and social approaches. History came to be viewed as a narrative with many goals, some of which deeply biased.

The doubts about history had immediate and profound effects on biblical scholarship. Lacking independent confirmation of events as told in the Bible, scholars by droves began to wonder about the certainties achieved earlier. In America, the intersection between the Bible's and the scholar's version of history continues to slip. Whereas two generations ago scholars began a verifiable history of Israel with the patriarchs, today they are arguing about the historicity of Solomon.

Amazingly enough, rather than driving us to despair this narrowing of the historical portals invites us to find other ways to penetrate the world of the Hebrews. There is now a willingness to put aside old methods, to work interdisciplinarily, and to adopt multiple strategies for solving a problem. In this atmosphere, rather than focusing on what exactly happened in Israel there is now a desire to better understand what Israel imagined happened in her past. One way of arriving at such an understanding is a sharper appreciation of the role Israel's God was given in shaping that history.

Yet, I must not end on such a note, for people of faith sometimes misunderstand the implication of dealing with a history of Israel that cannot be authenticated in all its details with what Scripture tells us. Once, a very great scholar, Father Roland de Vaux of the École Biblique in Jerusalem, was quoted to say, "If the historical faith of Israel is not founded in history, such faith is erroneous, and therefore, our faith is also."[46] I think such a conclusion is very drastic. To begin with, most of our arguments about the disjunction between what the Bible says happened and what we think happened is based on lack of supportive argument, textual or archeological. So, we must keep in mind the important principle that the absence of evidence is no evidence of absence. A discovery of an archive from the monarchic period could do wonders in a restoring faith in our sources.

Second, historians and archeologists are of course charged with recreating what really happened in history; but, as often as not, they are also in the business of revising each other's work. Witness the hot debates that are unending about the historicity of events, not just for the Old Testament, but even also for the New. So, as a second principle, I would personally not entrust historians and

---

[46]   Cited from Finkelstein and Silberman 2001: 34.

archeologists with final arbitration on matters that go beyond historical truths.

Finally, we must confront the fact that what Israel wanted most to communicate through its literature is given to us in forms and constructs that are largely impervious to historical appraisal. Israel gloated over its discovery of God and over its adoption of a superior code of behavior, calling on nations to exemplify divinely inspired truths. Israel did not just tell us about great acts of God, such as the splitting of the Red Sea or halting the sun over Gibeon; but it revealed the secret of its faith through hundreds of conversations between God and ordinary folks who, by hearkening to God's voice, achieved extraordinary ends. Such dialogues are, of course, beyond the capacity of archeology or history to authenticate. So, as a third principle, let me suggest therefore that whether or not Israel told its past accurately should not be a measure of its capacity to reach spiritual truth. Rather, we should stand in awe of Israel for being unequaled among its neighbors in its ability to discover the logic of monotheism and in its courage to broadcast that discovery as a historical truth.

In the third and final Chuen King lecture, we will talk about how it did so.

A Response to Lecture Two

Craig Y. S. HO

B. Th. (Alliance Bible Sem., HK), B. D. (SEAGST), Ph. D. (Edinburgh)
Assistant Professor, Department of Religion and Philosophy,
Hong Kong Baptist University

The Problem of Historicity in Hebrew Historiography and How to Cope with It as Christians
A Response
"On Hebrew History"

Craig Ho

I thank Prof. Sasson for updating our historical knowledge of the Hebrew people – however little we actually know. Prof. Sasson has not just shown us the poverty of our historical knowledge of the Hebrew Bible, he has also pointed out some exciting development in new historical tools and new discoveries. We have to keep in mind that he was not speaking about the history of another people but the ancient history of his own people. I appreciate the kind of critical rigor and openness he has adopted for the study of a history of which he is a part. The Hebrew Bible is the first part and in fact in quantitative term the main portion of our Christian scriptures. I think we need the same kind of openness and critical spirit he has demonstrated – if we want to learn something that is hopefully plausible and not just to believe something to be true without bothering about its likelihood of being true. In this response, I want first to discuss the necessity of critical approach to the Bible and then proceed to the problem of the relationship between faith and history, and finally to draw implications for Christians.

1. ON THE CRITICAL ENQUIRY OF THE HEBREW PEOPLE

Prof. Sasson in this lecture just delivered approaches the history of the Hebrew people in the Bible as a (modern) historian who requires "the testimony of at least two witnesses" (p. 42). This is a very important and common methodological rule, usually assumed rather than expressed, followed by all biblical scholars in the historical-critical tradition.[1] The problem to which he addresses in his paper can therefore be reformulated thus: in the lack of a second (literary) witness for most of the stories about the Hebrew people, how much of them can be accepted as historically plausible? To this question, his answer is very simple and straightforward: very little.

However, it is entirely possible that a single witness may still be reporting truth. As Prof. Sasson urges in the conclusion of his paper that "we must keep in mind that the absence of evidence is no evidence of absence." The reason why a historian would not commit total trust to a single witness' report has nothing to do with the intrinsic trustworthiness of the report but is based on a methodological principle. The trustworthiness of a biblical account, for a historian, is not to be believed, but must be substantiated by external or independent evidence. "External" in the present context usually means extra-biblical.

Yet for many if not most biblical stories that read like historical accounts independent witnesses are not available. This lack of a second witness/independent evidence does not, of course, prevent us from believing the truthfulness of the report of a single witness. But as soon as one believes something without external

---

[1]   For a defense of the critical approach, see John Barton, "Historical-critical Approaches", in John Barton, ed., *The Cambridge Companion to Biblical Interpretation* (Cambridge, 1998), pp. 9-20.

evidence, one is forfeiting the duty of the historian. The historian may assume various things in a historical explanation but one thing (s)he would not do is to believe the truth of an account purported to be history – that is something to be substantiated, not believed.

Furthermore, there is an interesting logical asymmetry in historical analysis: although an account should not be accepted as trustworthy without independent witnesses, it is possible to demonstrate its untrustworthiness just by internal analysis, e.g. by showing that an historical narrative contains internal contradictions or inconsistent claims, or claims that contradicts what is well known from other sources. That is, while historical reliability needs independent witness to substantiate, historical unreliability does not.[2] Internal incoherence is sometimes enough to discourage acceptance of biblical accounts at face value. Historical reliability of the Hebrew Bible will be further undermined if it can be shown that biblical historiography is tendentious or biased, which is often the case because the biblical material was produced or edited by supporters of the Davidic dynasty, i.e. the southerners, for whom the northern dynasties were illegitimate and the northern religion an apostasy.[3]

---

[2] One obvious internal difficulties that Prof. Sasson has pointed out is that chronology and genealogy of the Hebrew people are based on unrealistic or favoured numbers. They can therefore not be used to construct a time frame for Hebrew history.

[3] There is a tendency in the Former Prophets to Samaritanize the northerners. In the judgment against the northerners ("the people of Israel") in 2 Kgs 17, one accusation against them is that "they built for themselves high places ... (v. 9) ... which the Samaritans had made (v. 29)." The first appearance of "Samaritans" in the Hebrew Bible is found here!

It is true that biblical historians lived in pre-scientific or pre-critical times; they did not share our modern idea of what qualifies to be called "history." It may be unfair to them to expect their "histories," written more than two thousands years ago, to comply with our requirements. On the other hand, we are not pre-moderns and it is only appropriate that we evaluate ancient documents using critical methodology, which is also used in other disciplines and has produced very fruitful results.

2. ON FAITH AND HISTORY / FACTS

Critical enquiry, by definition, discourages faith in the biblical account of Israel's history. I can happily agree with Prof. Sasson's critique of the Albright school of biblical archaeology – they probably read too much of their faith in the letters of the Bible into the speechless evidence. It seems to me that they were more anxious than the biblical authors to proclaim the Bible as "historically trustworthy." It seems to me that Prof. Sasson has successfully shown "how little we actually know or can confirm about Israel's origin or real history." For the people of faith, the important question is this: how much of historicity is required for sound faith. This question, however, is only mildly discussed in his conclusion, which is meant, I suppose, to reduce the shock the audience might have felt from realizing how much of what have taken for granted in Hebrew history "is based on lack of supportive argument, textual or archaeological." Unfortunately there is not much I can do either!

Yet in reporting recent discoveries, it seems that after all we do know something, though not as much or as certain as before, about the ancient past of the Hebrews. It seems to me that historians may now know better, but hardly more about ancient Israel. The consolation I have got from his lecture is that the new tools may not generate stronger faith in biblical history but have accumulated bit by bit evidence of a better picture that does say that some of the Hebrew history did happen. We may not know more, but of the little we know, they are better than our previous knowledge – that is the rationale of biblical scholarship: we want to know better, not just more.

Near the end of his paper, he tackled the inevitable problem that would interest but sometimes frustrates us most: the relationship between faith and history. If the biblical portrayal of the Hebrew people cannot be taken at face value, how about the biblical religion? Prof. Sasson says, "I would personally not entrust historians and archeologists with final arbitration on matters that go beyond historical truths." I take this strategy of his to mean that theological truths cannot be decided by historical/archeological means. Previous optimism in archeological support of biblical history might have been motivated by a desire to base faith on historical certainty.[4] Now if such a certainty does not exist, upon where should we base our faith? If Father de Vaux's insistence that Israel's faith must be founded in history is not necessary, how should faith and history be related? My solution to this problem is this. All histories were written in retrospect when past events were selected and interpreted from a certain perspective. Such a perspective is a framework of meaning that relates a certain

---

[4]   Very much like the logical-positivists' attempt to found meaningful statements upon sense-data, the "atom" of history!

set of individual events and assigns cause-effect sequences to them. Such a framework of meaning is actually the interpretation imposed by the historian upon the events. Interpretations are not derivable from meaningless events; instead they come from the mind of the historian.[5]

Theology or faith in God is also a kind of framework of meaning. In other words, in the actual process of history writing, (theological) interpretation came first and shaped the historical accounts. Events in themselves have no connections or meanings if not interpreted. Historians cannot interpret a set of events if they do not have pre-conceived interpretation first! In other words, faith in God or theology came first in the actual writing of the narrative books in the Hebrew Bible.[6] Although biblical narratives put on historical dresses, they should more accurately be described as historicized theological convictions with some if not most of the historical details being fictions.[7] Without prior theological conviction no part of biblical history that mentions YHWH would have been written. Israel's theological account of their national fate is not founded in history. Instead theology shaped Israel's historical consciousness and then generated its historiography.

---

[5]   The same process happens in scientific reasoning. A hypothesis comes suddenly to the mind of the (well-trained) scientist to enable him/her to explain physical events. It is a mistake to think that scientific theories are based upon observations or inductive reasoning. See Karl Popper, *Conjectures and Refutations, the Growth of Scientific Knowledge* (London, 1972).

[6]   "Narrative books" is a better term to describe what we call historical books in the Hebrew Bible, see Iain Provan, "The Historical Books of the Old Testament" in John Barton, op. cit., pp. 198–211.

[7]   I have in mind the mirror images of Joseph (Gen. 39) and Amnon (2 Sam. 13), which can be shown by literary analysis to be composed using similar/identical phrases/motifs/story structure.

The belief that Israel's religion is a "historical faith," i.e. a faith anchored to/or generated from Yahweh's historical acts in history seems to me to be more a confessional characterization of biblical history than an accurate description of how this history came into being. Without prior faith in Yahweh, historical events could not have generated theological interpretation of events in which Yahweh's acts were not obvious to the naked eyes – unless one assumes that Yahweh acted observably differently then than now. With faith in Yahweh, even "speechless" events can be understood "as if" Yahweh was actively involved – through the eyes of the faithful and without exception with the theological hindsight of the guardians of Israel's tradition. I am afraid this way of putting faith over history (or spirit over letter, in St. Paul's words) is not quite compatible with the kind of positivistic theology that is very popular in fundamentalist/evangelical circles, which requires a solid epistemological foundation (e.g. an infallible bible or an insistence of the priority of history over theology) to support faith. I think the results of recent historical/archaeological researches on the Hebrew people reported in Prof. Sasson's lecture on Hebrew history expose the illusion of basing faith upon solid knowledge – the same illusion of a kind of philosophy that has long been dead.[8]

---

[8] The once fashionable logical positivism claims that statements that are not verifiable (in principle at least) are non-sensual and therefore metaphysical and that science is based on empirical statements, which in turn are based on sense data, i.e. direct knowledge. The idea that science is a set of empirical statements that have been verified and therefore based on solid knowledge has been found to be an illusion in the final analysis. Philosophers of science nowadays have agreed that even the most truth-like scientific theories are but well tested hypotheses/conjectures that may one day be superseded by better hypotheses.

3. PEOPLE OF THE BOOK?

Prof. Sasson's lecture would certain touches the nerve of our (evangelical) faith with respect to the Bible. Most of us Christians in Hong Kong were brought up in conservative churches that still preach biblical inerrancy. Now it may seem wise, safe and "politically correct" for biblical scholars who want to stay in the evangelical circles not to touch those nerves lest the heart takes over the mind in heated discussions, to say the least. It is, however, clearly self-deceiving if a responding scholar from the evangelical tradition facing Prof. Sasson's "minimal" approach to archaeological evidence now widely accepted by careful and responsible historians does not consider its implications for the audience who are virtually all from the evangelical tradition. I want therefore to put forward the following points that take the results of Prof. Sasson's paper into consideration to help formulate a solution to the problem of "how little we actually know or can confirm about Israel's origin or real history":

(1) What do we mean when we as Christians say, "I believe in the Bible"? None of the ancient creeds includes such an article of faith. I think the reason is quite simple – not all the Jews/Christians have the same Bible in the first century.[9] An article of faith surrounding the Bible could not possibly be formed without a canonized collection of scriptures and before it can be widely read by individual Christians. Thus before Luther's Reformation and the invention of the printing

---

[9]   Those in Palestine favoured the Hebrew Bible but for the Greek speaking Diaspora and the first Christians, their favourite was the LXX. The fixing of the New Testament Canon is partly helped by the attempt to correct Marcion's error.

press – the success of the former depended very much on the latter – for a very long time the Bible belonged to the Church (authority) and not to individual believers. The believer was told to believe in the Church and what she said about the Bible. The slogan *Sola Scriptura* is very much the product of Luther's attempt to replace a subjective authority – the Pope – by an objective one. (Yet even Luther had difficulties with some biblical books!) Paradoxically, the Old Testaments of the Roman Catholic Church and the Eastern Orthodox Church are closer to the one read by the first century Christians than the Protestant OT (without the Apocrypha).

(2) The two pictures of Hebrew history as "reported" in the Hebrew Bible and as reconstructed by historians based on archaeological artifacts are very different and incompatible. They simply cannot be true at the same time. What should we do? Do we just stick to the Bible whatever biblical scholars say? We may do this but I think we should not because it is the intellectual duty of an educated person to be at least reasonably sure that what (s)he believes corresponds to the best evidence available to her/him.

(3) For those of us who have some interest in biblical scholarship, I would think that with respect to Hebrew history, it makes sense to accept what seems to you the best available result of biblical scholarship and be reminded that all theories are the products of the human mind and are only well-argued hypotheses. We should also be tolerant to those who hold different views and be open to unexpected findings.

(4) For those of us who have not yet appreciated the relevance of biblical scholarship or are not "interested" in historical reconstructions, or if you want to stick to biblical inerrancy at "whatever the cost." there is nothing to apologize. Keep your simple faith in "What the Bible says" as long as you can but when one day you suddenly no longer be able to take the Bible at face value, do not panic, that is not the end of the world. The exciting world of biblical scholarship at different levels is waiting for you to find out more. Take as much as you can digest!

(5) The sources of our knowledge of God are multifold: (1) canonized traditions inherited (the Old Testament) or preserved (i.e. the New Testament) by the church, (2) non-canonized traditions that include writings of the ancient fathers and modern interpreters/expositors of the gospel, and (3) personal experience of God. The Bible points to God's words and acts "as" experienced or witnessed by the Hebrew people and the first Christians *in the past.* However, we believe in a living God, whose reality does not depend on written documents.

(6) Critical scholarship is a very important contribution of the 18th century Enlightenment in Europe and have affected biblical scholarship ever since. We cannot of course go back to a pre-critical period, and the result of critical historical study has helped us to see more clearly that in final analysis our faith rests entirely on God rather than anything else. It is our faith in God that enables us to appreciate the inspiration and authority of the Bible.

THIRD LECTURE

On the Origins of the Hebrew God
and of the Hebrew Faith in God

THIRD LECTURE
ON THE ORIGINS OF THE HEBREW GOD
and of the Hebrew Faith in God

THE ISSUES

The topic of my third lecture is the search for the origins of the Hebrew God. Before examining what scholarship has to say about the origins of the Hebrew God, let me briefly review the main points of the previous two presentations. In the first lecture, I looked at how the Hebrew narrators presented history, suggesting that their goal for writing about their past was not limited to recounting exactly what had happened. Rather, conventions, themes, and a predilection for narrating history through a series of biographies controlled the shape of that past that was worth preserving. The resulting biographies were linked through the role God plays in directing the movements of all concerned.

In the second lecture, I spoke about the problem scholarship encounters when the biblical version of history cannot be confirmed through extra-biblical testimony, either archaeological or documentary. I suggested that, because of the difficulty in harmonizing two versions of Israel's past, many scholars have focused on understanding what Israel imagined to have happened in her past. To understand how Israel envisioned her history requires a sharper appreciation of the role her God was granted in shaping that history. In this lecture then, I will tackle three mutually instructive issues:

1. What do scholars have to say about the origin of the Hebrew God, especially in comparison with what we have learned about the gods of the ancient Near East?
2. What was distinctive in Israel's worship of that God.
3. What can we say about the idea of a unique God.

A. THE SEARCH FOR THE HEBREW GOD
1. A Newtonian Universe

Until the eighteenth century in Europe, there was no sustained search for the Hebrew God. Since the Renaissance, people had generally conceded the cultivation of the mind to the Greeks, the control of society to the Romans, the revelation of the only true God to Israel, and the inspiration for true salvation to the Gospels. The major issue then was how to understand the functioning of the universe, and in this endeavor, the most avid cosmographers were the theologians and the philosophers. Only a couple of centuries earlier it had been proven that the sun and not the earth was the center of that universe. A shift had also occurred from an Aristotelian, purpose-oriented (teleological) world that was guided by a divine mind to a Newtonian formulation in which the universe runs itself like a clock, obeying mechanical laws. In this Enlightenment atmosphere, God was more or less retired from active duty.

Although it had antecedents, our own story about the search for the Hebrew God picks up in the mid-eighteenth century, when Europe began to dominate the continents militarily and economically, and so increasingly thought of itself as the pinnacle of human achievement. There was the certitude that European religious beliefs, protected and nurtured by an approving God, were destined to prevail worldwide. This conviction anticipated a Darwinian tenet that the fittest is destined to succeed. Accompanying political dominance, therefore, was a missionary zeal to bring Christianity to cultures that were not raised on biblical verities. To ensure success, there was a drive, sustained by scholars and missionaries, to better understand the religious beliefs that were being supplanted. Partly in the fulfillment of this effort, the writings of great cultures such as those in China and India were studied for clues and field research was undertaken to collect religious testimony from cultures that did not write. It was natural, too, to consult the writings of the Greeks and the Romans, cultures that had been absorbed into Christianity when it triumphed in the early first millennium.

But there was also a parallel drive to penetrate sacred Scripture itself, to discover from it something about the verities that so inspired the Hebrews. It seemed logical, therefore, to focus on a God who, despite many setbacks, eventually inspired Israel to discover the logic of monotheism and gave it courage to broadcast this insight as a historical truth. Who was this Hebrew God and how did Israel and this god discover each other.

B. A GOD OF MANY NAMES
1. YHWH

Throughout antiquity, it was believed that *nomen est omen*, meaning that the names given to people, places, or gods, gave clues about their role and destiny. In the Hebrew Bible, a good deal of ingenuity was expanded to establish a linkage between name and fate. Such a linkage was also suggested for the private name applied to God, YHWH. His name was written with just four consonants—*Yod, he, waw, he*—not because Hebrews delighted in owning unpronounceable words, but because the scribes of the regions could write whatever they wished without using vowels. Many personal names of the period were crafted as verbal sentences, such as "God judges" (Jehosaphat) and "God has given" (Natanyahu, Jonathan), and in such cases YHWH could occur in such shortened forms as *yô-, yehô-, -yawû* and *-yahû*. The four-consonant name, the "Tetragammaton" as it is termed in Greek, is presumed to be based on the verb hāyâ, "to exist," although the linkage is not certain. Unfortunately, there is no tradition that reliably tells us how to pronounce the Tetragammaton, and the name "Jehovah," artificially created from the four consonants and broadly used in Europe and America, has no basis in antiquity.[47]

---

[47] For Jews the Tetragammaton was too holy for pronunciation by all but the High Priest, and only during the most awesome of moments. According the Mishnah (Succa IV, 5) during the liturgy for the Succoth festival, the priests intoned an obscure phrase ʾanî wahô hôšî ʿâ-nnâ which, because it paralleled Ps 118:25's ʾannāʾ YHWH hôšîʿâ-nnāʾ, may be recast as ʾn ywhw, so giving us *Yôhû as one pronunciation for God's name that was prevalent during the last days of the Temple. But note that in one Greek manuscript from Qumran (4Q210, fragment 20,4) YHWH of Leviticus 4:27 is given phonetically as *Iao*; see Vermes 1998: 490.

At all other times, pious Jews substituted the word "my lord," ʾădōnay whenever they needed to pronounce YHWH. Later, when vowels were added to consonants to stabilize the reading of Scripture, the vowels from "my lord" were placed under the 4 consonants, to alert people against a sacrilegious pronunciation. Those who did not know about the convention behind this vocalization came up with the misguided hybrid YEHOWAH, hence "Jehovah," attested to as early as the twelfth, but more persistently since the sixteenth, century. Though misbegotten, Jehovah is now a fine word and can be found listed in dictionaries and serves as entry in such encyclopedias as the Britannica. (The same route was taken by the English "Ye" which is based on misreading a symbol for the ligature "th" as in the article "the.")

The Hebrews themselves were curious about their God's name. In Exodus 3:13-15 we are told that when Moses tried to escape the burden God was imposing on him, he asked "Suppose I come before the people of Israel and I tell them that their ancestral god sent me to you, what if they ask me what is his name, what can I tell them? God replied, tell them 'EHYEH ASHER EHYEH,' adding, tell them 'EHYEH' sent me to you . . . This is my name from time immemorial and this is how I am recalled from one generation to another" (see also Revelation 1:4,11, 17).

The answer may have satisfied Moses who, in fact, never depended on this password for entry among his kin. The Egyptians he met, too, were far more impressed by his clever magic than by the name of the god that gave him his mission. Still, for us, the explanation that God gives Moses remains enigmatic. Presuming that the name is based on the verb hāyâ, "to exist," we can render the phrase, "I am who I am," or "I am what I am," "I am what I create," "I create what I am," and the like.[48]

Not surprisingly, Semitic specialists are also divided on how to understand the meaning of the name YHWH, and it does not help that we do not know how it was pronounced. Even if we agree that it is based on the verb hāyâ and that this verb has to be understood as the Hebrew/Aramaic for "to be" (by no means obvious propositions), a vocalized form of YHWH can suggest

---

[48] See Freedman 1960. The phrase was especially rich in potential meanings for medieval mystics; see Goetschel 1987.

diverse translations, such as "He is," or "He will be."[49] But there are fine scholars who treat it as a causative (athough the causative stem is not found for this verb in our Hebrew dictionaries), arriving at such explanations as "I create what I am," "I am what I create," or even as the wordy "It is He who creates What Comes into Existence" (Albright 1968: 148).[50]

Be that as it may, this private name of the Hebrew God figures in the most famous article of faith crafted by Israel: šĕmaᶜ yiśrāʾēl YHWH ʾĕlōhênû YHWH ʾeḥād" (Deut 6:4), commonly rendered as "Listen Israel, The Lord is our God, The Lord is One." Yet this seventh-century BCE credo, crafted when Israel controlled its own destiny, proclaims the incomparability, the supremacy, the lonesomeness if you will, of that God; but not his uniqueness.[51] Another passage from the same book could even imply that God has assigned the sun and the moon to be worshiped; but not by Israel (Deut 4:19).[52] Indeed, Israel undermines its conviction about

---

[49] Some scholars (for example Knauf 1984) seek an etymology from Arabic, with meanings as diverse as "to grieve," "to desire," or "to hurt."

[50] The discussion on the name and pronunciation of YHWH is vast, see conveniently the dictionaries and encyclopedias under entries such as "God (names of)," "Adonay," and "YHWH". See also the sane overviews by de Vaux (1978: 338-357) and the article of Freedman and O'Connor (1980). Some scholars find the association of YHWH with such appellatives as ṣĕbāʾôt ("Hosts") and such nouns as ʾĕlōhîm (God/gods) to convey the real meaning behind YHWH, "He who brings the (heavenly) hosts into being," and "He who brings the gods into being;" see Halpern 1993: 525; L'Heureux 1981: 43, both depending on Cross 1973: 60-75.

[51] The phrase šĕmaᶜ yiśrāʾēl is found only in Deuteronomy where it is similarly exhortatory in 9:1, 20:3, 27:9 (see also 6:3). The phrase YHWH ʾeḥad surprisingly enough occurs only in one other place in Scripture (Zech 14:9). On how to parse this phrase, see Bord and Hamidović 2002. Geller 2000: 290-296 (with bibliography) in fact ties the phrase to Exod 6:5 translating, "Hear, Israel, since Yahweh our God, Yahweh is one (i.e. supreme), you shall love ..." (p. 293).

[52] "And when you look up to the sky and see the sun, the moon and the stars, the full heavenly host, you must not be lured into bowing down to them or worshiping what the LORD your God has allotted to all the nations under heaven." On this passage and its implication, see Weinfeld 1991: 206-207.

the uniqueness of its God, when it chants mî khāmōkhâ bā ʾēlîm YHWH, "Who compares to you among the gods, Lord?" (Exod 15:11), when it praises YHWH as the "God of gods" (Josh 22:22; Ps 50:1), when the first of its Ten Commandments privileges YHWH over any other god (Exod 20:2-5), when its prophet Micah (4:5) confesses, "Just as every nation acts in the name of its god, we also act in the name of our god YHWH, now and forever," or when its bards assign victories to foreign gods (2 Kings 3:27).[53] That prophets found it necessary to warn about the seductive powers of other gods speaks volumes about Israel's belief in their effectiveness, if not also their existence.

This complex information on Hebraic attachment to the notion of a single god has played a major role in the scholarly examination of the origins of Israel's God and the nature of Israel's faith in that God, a subject to which I now want to turn.

2. YHWH and The Documentary Hypothesis

The Hebrews did not invoke God only as YHWH, normally rendered "The LORD" in our translations. Rather, they called on him by several names, a few so obscure in meaning (let alone origins), that they continue to resist solution. Some were generic terms for a deity, such as El, equivalent to "god" with a small "g" and diverse expansion of that term through attributes, such as El-Elyon, "Loftiest God," and El-Olam "Eternal God." Elohim, a plural form of El, is very common. When applied to the Hebrew God,

---

[53] Even when this commandment (Exodus 20:3; Deuteronomy 5:7) is rendered "You shall have no other gods *besides Me*" (Tanakh; after a suggestion by W. F. Albright), the warning is against choosing rival gods (see NJB) rather than a declaration about their non-existence.

Elohim was always associated with a verbal form in the singular, and so it was understood as a vessel for godhood. In our translations, Elohim occurs as "God." Other names, such as Shaddai, "Almighty," and YHWH Sebaoth, "LORD of Hosts," are elusive enough that people write books about their meanings. Many are simply epithets that happened to be used in Scripture, for example, Adon ("Master") and, ironically enough, Baal ("Possessor").

This very rich repertoire of names and epithets seemed to betray multiple inspirations and so launched the first queries about God's nature. Researchers sought their evidence within the Hebrew Bible itself. In the late eighteenth century, even before the cultures of the ancient Near East acquired voices through the decipherment of their scripts, it was suggested that the two most commonly used names for God, YHWH and Elohim betrayed the presence of two distinct modes of conceiving of God. From this germ scholars developed an elaborate scheme, eventually labeled the *Documentary Hypothesis*, as discussed in the first lecture. For the purpose if this lecture, we recall that Julius Wellhausen, using the achievements of historians of religion in his day, divided the theological history of Israel into three major periods. For him the patriarchal period was too nebulous to chart; but he thought that until almost the end of the monarchic period—let us say the seventh century BCE– worship in Israel was loosely based, albeit centered around YHWH, with many religious temples, local priests, and a Canaanite-influenced mode of sacrifice. Around 630 BCE, King Josiah of Judah initiated feverish reforms that centralized worship in Jerusalem and advocated a passionate covenant with Yahweh.

According to this theory, the final phase began after the Exile (around 500 BCE), and it involved a priestly group eager to codify religious behavior into rigid class segmentation and exclusivist behavior.

Wellhausen's brilliant thesis has had its share of criticism: from scholars who no longer shared his patently regressive exposition of religious institutions; from Christians who were troubled by its presumption of a human (rather than a divinely-centered) inspiration; and from Jews for implicitly suggesting a desiccation of its spiritual heritage. It was shown, too, that the thesis he championed depended on culling information from one context to make it serve another. Moreover, on the few occasions in recent years when archaeology was called to judge elements of the thesis, it has not confirmed them. For example, we now know that despite what Hebrew sources tell us about the consolidation of worship exclusively in the Jerusalem temple during the late monarchic period, excavations have produced fully functioning temples elsewhere. There is even debate now on whether the "J" material, to which Wellhausen gave precedence, may in fact be much later than previously argued. If so, it can turn his conclusions upside down; indeed in the hands of some recent scholars, it already has.[54]

In arguing his thesis, too, Wellhausen depended on inner-biblical exegesis, largely ignoring the burgeoning information

---

[54] See, De Pury's good overview, 1992.

accumulating from deciphered Egyptian, Mesopotamian, Anatolian, and Canaanite. Even during his lifetime, this evidence was increasingly demonstrating is that the Hebrews made their God behave like one of the despised deities of Israel's neighbors— and vice versa. For example, a stone monument found in 1868 at Dhiban (Jordan) gives a (pseudo-)autobiographic account of the triumphs of the late ninth-century BCE king Mesha of Moab against the kings of Israel. Mesha tells how his god Chemosh, once angry against his people, turned gracious and allowed them to destroy their Israelite foes. In doing so, Mesha uses vocabulary and formulae that could have been written by a fervent worshiper of the Hebrew God.[55]

3. Extra-biblical YHWH

What have we learned about YHWH in nearly two centuries since the great decipherments? To be perfectly honest about it, the archaeological and epigraphic evidence has muddled our knowledge of YHWH and his origins. We have so far found no credible information about the worship of a god by the same name outside of Israel's borders. From the early second millennium (so when the Hebrews had not yet gelled into a discernable entity), we have names of people and places, such as Yahwi-El, Yawi-Addu that have been interpreted as mentioning the Hebrew God. We also find in Canaanite myth an obscure allusion to a son of

---

[55] The Mesha stela is widely quoted, for example Pritchard 1969 [= *ANET*³], 320-321. A readable study (with nice bibliography) is Smelik 1991: 29-50, 171-172. A good overview can be found in Dearman and Mattingly 1992. A recent study that reviews its import on Hebrew narrative style is Rainey 2001b.

Baal named YW.[56] While scholars continue to fight with passion about whether such tidbits are evidence of the knowledge of YHWH among non-Hebrews, in truth even if people in antiquity were found to worship a deity named YHWH, that god was certainly not the only one they worshiped or proclaimed. Consequently, the way they assessed his nature and the covenant they had with him may have been nothing like what was prevalent in Israel.

But what about the extra-biblical mention of a YHWH who is linked specifically with Israel? We now have almost fifty mentions of YHWH in extra-biblical texts and they show that monotheistic faith was soft, with syncretism and heterodoxy prevailing among the larger segment of the population even after the Exile. Israel's YHWH is mentioned earliest in the Mesha inscription of the ninth century, and he is treated with the same indignity by the Moabites as Hebrews treated foreign gods. We also have documents from Jews living in Egypt during the fifth century BCE, and they show that they worshiped Anat-YHW, apparently a fusing into one godhead Yahweh and the Canaanite goddess Anat.[57] But we were not prepared for what was recently recovered from an obscure site in the Sinai peninsula (Kuntillet ʿAjrud). Fragments of large pottery jars were found, a number of which had votive invocations that sought the blessing of "YHWH of Samaria (or of Teman) and

---

[56] Finet 1993. A good survey of the material is found in Weippert 1976-80. On linking Ugaritic YW with YHWH, see de Moor 1986; on Yahweh in topographical lists, see Astour 1979.

[57] See van der Toorn 1992; Some scholars suggest that the Anat element is symbolic for something like "providence" or "sign," hence "Sign of Yahweh"; see Maier 1992: 226.

of his Asherah." With the inscriptions were inked grotesque pictures of a (possibly) sexually aroused bull ogling a cow and her calf. Behind him stand an attendant and a lyre-playing musician.[58] Needless to say scholars are still in a tizzy about the implication of this hoard of evidence likely from the early 8th century BCE, so long before the Exile and the end of the monarchic period. Some scholars are certain that the material proves that Israel was religiously a child of its time. Others think that we have recovered a sectarian group with less than full monotheistic attachment to YHWH. Many were intrigued by the association of YHWH and Asherah, an association that is repeated in another recently found inscription, this one from near Hebron, so from the heartland of Judah.[59] Asherah was a well known goddess, wife of El, head of the Canaanite pantheon, and frequently portrayed there as a tease. Whether at Kuntilet ʿAjrud she was YHWH's consort, a feminine manifestation of his power (such as was the *shekhinah* in medieval Judaism), or as a representation of his presence (as a wooden post) is currently widely debated, with good arguments on all sides.[60]

To summarize thus far: Antiquity is not especially generous in

---

[58] See Meshel 1992 (with bibliography).
[59] On this inscription see Lemaire 1977.
[60] On Asherah and her cult, see Meshel 1992, Day 1994, Emerton 1984 and Hadley 1987, 1994, 2000. That a personal suffix (here: "his") is not normally attached to personal names (here: Asherah) is taken as strong argument against "asherah" being a consort; see Tigay 1986: 27 n. 34; but see Freedman's playful opinion on the matter (1987). We note that when Elijah confronted, bested, and slaughtered 450 priests of Baal on Mount Carmel, he did not harm 400 priests of Asherah (1 Kings 18). On a connection of the evidence with the kingdom of Israel, see Meshel 1994. Wiggins (2001) reopens the question of what is an "asherah."

revealing secrets. So, despite our rummaging into the dustbins of history, as yet we have not located reliable testimony to establish who first worshiped YHWH and where. This failure should not shock us. The Hebrews came relatively late into our vision, no earlier than the 12th century BCE, when many of their neighbors were already old cultures. It would even take a few more centuries for these neighbors to notice them in a significant way, so minor a player were they in political history. I fear, therefore, that how the Hebrews came to YHWH as the sponsor of their destiny remains a question for the philosopher and the theologian rather than the historian and philologist.[61]

C. THE SEARCH FOR YAHWISM
1. Yahwism and Other Near Eastern Theologies

If the search for YHWH has not yielded a definite answer on the origin(s) of the Hebrew god, has scholarship been more successful in locating the roots of Yahwism? Specifically, has it tracked down those elements of belief and worship that made the Hebrew faith in YHWH so distinctive?[62] The aim for us is to move away from the many notions the ancients, including the Hebrews, shared about the gods; for example, their eternal nature, their capacity to create, to hurt, and to heal; their control of the cosmos and of destiny; their eagerness to take sides, to win battles for their favorites, and to inflict defeat on them when teaching lessons. Here too, the aim is to set aside speculation about

---

[61] See the remarks of L'Heureux, 1981.
[62] This issue must not be confused with problems associated with identifying the Yahwist, the latter being the "author/editor" of the "J" document, according to the Documentary Hypothesis.

differences in practices and in institutions where, superficially, Israel seems to be listening to a different drumbeat than heard by its neighbors. Without entering into detail, we can say now that Israel was not unique in shunning worshiping through an idol or a representation of its god, either anthropomorphically or symbolically.[63] Too, prophets galore tried to inspire or admonish kings, with equal success or failure.[64] We have also found that justice and law were thought divinely inspired throughout the ancient world, with explicit covenants charting the relationship between gods and humankind.[65] The distinction between the Hebrew's God of history and the polytheist's god of nature, once widely-disseminated in scholarship, has been laid to rest a generation ago.[66] Some of Israel's less charming practices, we are relieved to say, were also known elsewhere. For example, we are learning

---

[63] See Sasson (forthcoming).

[64] The literature on ancient near eastern prophecy is immense. A recent good monograph is by Nissinen 2000; see also the overview of Vanderkam 1995.

[65] See Buccellati 1995.

[66] This is the thesis of Albrektson 1967. His thesis has engendered an enormous reaction. See Saggs' chapter, "The Divine in History," (1978: 64-91) for a sympathetic reception and a critique of critics. Recently some dramatic examples from the ancient Near East have come to buttress this thesis. One of them is the text we label "The Sin of Sargon and Sennacherib's 'Last Will' " (Tadmor, et al.) in which the sins of the father are rehearsed. Already from the Mari archives a full millennium earlier, we have the reflection of a king (so not a theologian), conveyed in a letter (so not a theological tractate). King Yarim-Lim of Yamkhad explains to his son-in-law Zimri-Lim why he must not anger the god Addu (a storm god) by extraditing leaders who had sought shelter in his country. In doing so, he finds instructive the fate of his own father Sumu-Epukh:

> Sumu-Epukh...came close to the kingdom that the god Addu had given King Samsi-Addu. But Sumu-Epukh, my father, did not live until old age: because he attacked the land... that Addu had given Samsi-Addu, Addu killed him. Until now, Addu has not become angry with me. (After Whiting 1995.)

that the ḥerem, the emptying of land of its occupants as part of a Holy War, was invented neither by Joshua nor by his God.[67]

As far as we can tell, however, Israel was indeed unique in the ancient world to have the Sabbath. To sanctify it, Israel invented the week, a calendric unit that was unknown elsewhere.[68] We can say, too, that no other people circumcised their males at their second week of existence and no priesthood was as relentless in codifying food and purity taboos.[69] While all cultures of the ancient world gave credit to their gods for insisting on ethical and moral behavior, no other god but YHWH felt the need to regulate the most personal aspects of life, such as with whom to be intimate, what to wear, how to shave, whom to frequent, and what to think. To our discomfort, too, we find Israel practically alone in denying its women direct access to God.

No doubt, Israel ascribed every one of these practices to the

---

[67] Much has been written on this topic. For succinct reviews, see de Vaux 1997: 258-267. Lohfink (1997: 180-199) is especially careful with the vocabulary and review potential parallel from Greece, Rome (*devotio*) and ancient Europe. The classic study of von Rad, is now translated into English (von Rad, 1991), with a good review of the history of discussion (by B. C. Ollenburger) and a nice bibliography (by J. E. Sanderson). There is an excellent collection of articles on war in the ancient Near East that include a fine study by A. Lemaire, see Nehme 1999. N. Gottwald (1972: 942-944) succinctly challenged Von Rad's opinion. The exact meaning of the formula, *qiddeš milḥāmâ*, "to sanctify a battle" (Jeremiah 6:4, Joel 4:9, Micah. 3:5) is still in dispute.

[68] See Sasson 1992. The Assyrians of the early second millennium BCE may have known a seven-day period, but it had limited application; see veenhof 1995-1996.

[69] On circumcision as practiced in the ancient Near East, see Sasson 1966. Most good biblical dictionaries have entries on this topic, often with workable bibliographies.

will of its God; but so did other societies when explaining idiosyncratic communal behavior. What does eventually distinguish Yahwism from all other religious beliefs from antiquity is monotheism. If we can come to a reasonable explanation of how Israel arrived at its conviction on the uniqueness of its god we might compensate for our previous failure to pin down his origins. As it happens this was the issue around which a discipline called history of religion was sharpening its research skills during the 19th century, and it is still alive today.[70] So we need to backtrack before proceeding.

2. The History of Religion(s)

It might seem paradoxical that some of the same drives that led Wellhausen to crack the biblical text into distinct segments, J, E, D, and P, were also at work to solve the mystery of Hebrew monotheism. Implicit in their approach is a rejection of the biblical notion that monotheism was born when God sought out Abram just after he left Ur of the Chaldeans (Gen 12). As said above, the mass of information collected by missionaries, antiquarians, travelers, and scholars about the worship of the non-Christian forced introspection on Europeans, if only to delineate how their progression to the true God was grounded not just in history but also intellectually. Some thinkers proposed that monotheism was natural and primordial and that over the course of history people had degenerated spiritually. In this explanation, Israel was thought

---

[70]   Dietrich and Klopfenstein 1994; Porter 2000.

to have *rediscovered* monotheism; but its version remained incomplete until Christianity contributed a vehicle for redemption.[71] The dominant view, however, was much more evolutionist, proposing that humanity was moving from an animistic, nature-oriented worship, to an understanding of the divine that was elevated, ethical, and universal. The path taken covered eons in developing, and included at least the following progression: *animism*, the worship of natural phenomena such a storm, an oak, a lion; *polytheism*, the worship of gods with human shapes and emotions; *henotheism*, one god as all, during the moment of worship; *monolatry*, one god only, supreme within its own borders; *monocratism*, one deity, dominant everywhere.[72] Monotheism, was placed as the last stage; but to accommodate highly spiritual cultures, for example in China and in India, there were still demarcations to negotiate. Some were positive, such as *theistic*, personal, and ethical monotheism, often associated with the prophets, pre-muslim sages (ḥanif), and a few favored Greek philosophers; but others received less positive labels, such as *radical, uncompromising, absolute*, and *exclusive* monotheism, the last series often attributed to Jews, who were deemed too absolute in their theology.

---

[71] Another irony: Israel was also accused of having come to monotheism by instinct, so unlike the intellectual effort of Greece in charting philosophy; see Olender 1987: 348. The notion of primitive monotheism is best exemplified in the work of Wilhelm Schmidt's *Urmonotheismus* (1912-1955). It is interesting to note that in the historiography of religions, the natural approach was to assume a primitive monotheism that degenerated into polytheism. It was not until David Hume's *Natural History of Religion* (1757) and Charles de Brosses' *Du culte des dieux fétiches* (1760) that polytheism was placed at the head of a progressive spiritual enlightenment; see Schmidt 1912:50-52.

[72] A fine overview is the article "Religion," in the 11th edition of the *Encyclopaedia Britannica* (1910-1911). A brief bot insightful book on the subject is Olender 1992.

3. Monotheistic Inspirations in the Ancient Near East

How to deal with the evidence from the Hebrew Bible became a conundrum.[73] On the one hand there was no denying the Bible's powerful and single-minded pleas for the uniqueness of God, especially by the prophets. Yet, YHWH was depicted also as heavily territorial. We have the anecdote about Saul pursuing David so harshly, that David complained of being forced into a foreign land, and so potentially to the worship of foreign gods (1 Sam 26:17-20). Informed by their own time, the ideas and metaphors about God in the Bible present him as a male oriental potentate, brooking little opposition, exhibiting jealousies and petulance, and displaying favor and disapproval in predictably human fashion, creating a context for biblical religion that is at once exceedingly primitive, yet eerily sublime. How much of the Biblical gendering of YHWH as a male deity, with human emotions, can be attributed to the Hebrew language's difficulty with creating abstractions (see the First Lecture) and how much it depended on a pagan perspective of the divine became issues that are still unresolved in today's scholarship. Already in the past century, there was a readiness to ascribe the worship of YHWH to two levels. To the priests and elite of Israel were assigned a henotheistic or monocratic notion of YHWH, all powerful within his domain. The masses, however, were said to accept a less pristine theology that included a happily married God who never

---

[73] The angle from which to perceive the development of monotheism in Israel can vary radically, as recent works show: de Moor 1990, Goodman 1996, Gnuse 1997.

stopped competing with deities such as Baal and El.[74] The Kuntillet ᶜAjrud material only sharpened this last view.

Kenites. But what about monotheism as we have come to understand it? When did it dawn in Israel's past? In the 1860s, so before the avalanche of near eastern testimony, a theory was launched that credited monotheistic inspiration to the father-in-law of Moses. Reuel, who was also known as Jethro and Hobab, may have been a priest among the Kenites / Midianites tribes. (They are not nearly the same, but scholarship of the time was arguing that they were; Moore 1895, 34 n. ‡). Reuel, who was full of YHWH's praise and sacrificed to him, volunteered expert advice to Moses on how to govern the vast horde that exited Egypt (Exod 18). Largely on this testimony, Reuel was credited with inspiring Moses towards monotheism. More recently, tidbits from Egyptian sources and from excavations in the Sinai were woven (at Harvard) to buttress a hypothesis that Israel learned all about Yahwism from these tribes. This hypothesis has yet to be substantiated by actual sources.[75]

Assur and Aten. With the abundance of information streaming out of post-decipherment Egypt, Mesopotamia, Canaan, and Anatolia, the land of the Hittites, the task of evaluating Hebrew

---

[74] The terminology is loose, with "popular," "family," and "heterodox" religions serving scholars as a catch-alls for theologies and practices that are not purely Yahwistic. Needless to say almost all the textual material that is called upon to flesh out these aspects of Hebrew religion is extracted from the Hebrew Bible.

[75] A good (and sympathetic) review of the evidence is Halpern 1992. For a skeptical review of the same, see de Vaux 1978: 330-338.

monotheism became at once simpler and more complicated. Simpler, because these highly sophisticated cultures were unabashedly polytheistic; so we leisurely set out to describe how different Israel was in its worship of the unique God. More complicated, because a hymn, a prayer, an incantation, or a ritual can present a god under worship henotheistically, that is as towering over all others if not also unique. (Historians of religion labeled them "High Gods.") When this god was also the tutelary deity of a powerful nation-state, the tendency of ancient theologians was to magnify prestige by assimilating other divinities into him or her. This is what happened during the last years of the Assyrian Empire, when the exaltation of the god Assur was reaching completeness, and at the end of the Babylonian Empire, when King Nabonidus became fervent in his worship of the god Sin of Haran. There is now a broad literature by a very competent Assyriologist (Simo Parpola) arguing that Assyrian royal ideology, priestly theology, and mystery practices in the Assyrian capitals had resulted in a religion that is, despite its polytheistic trappings and the nurturing of countless other deities, was essentially monotheistic. Parpola has even found evidence of and esoteric theology that anteceded the Kabbalah by almost two millennia. It is difficult for me to accept such a flaccid notion of monotheism, for on its basis we can argue the same for the attachment of any priest to a specific shrine.[76]

---

[76] See his essay in Porter 1997. In fact, it would have been far more convincing to argue that Judaism of the Middle Ages had reverted to a form of mystical polytheism. See below.

Whether Egypt was the cradle of monotheism was also the subject of scholarly debates. At the dawn of its history, the 2nd Dynasty Pharaoh Peribsen tried to bolster the worship of the god Seth. This was around 2700 BCE, so much too early to link to Hebrew monotheism. However, during the 18th Dynasty, so around 1350 BCE, Akhnaten (the name has diverse spellings) promoted the worship of Aten (Aton). Because the events leading to the rise and fall of the god Aten under the sponsorship of this pharaoh teem with incredibly dramatic personalities and moves, because Atenism happened just as Israel was about to form, and because a circumstantial case can be made to attach Moses, directly or inspirationally, to Akhnaten's court, for the past century there has been a veritable industry to evaluate Akhnaten's monotheism and assessing its effect on Israel. My own notion is that Atenism, while an incredible leap toward monotheism, never made it there; if only because its chief sponsor, Akhnaten, believed himself also to be a god and had a high priest to worship him as such. His co-regent, Smenkare, had a name that glorified yet another god, Ra.[77] More importantly, Atenism had a very limited run, outlasting the death of Akhnaten by a handful of years, so that any direct connection between Atenism and Yahwism must be left to the imagination of novelists (Mika Waltari), film-makers (The Egyptian, 1954), psycho-historians (Sigmund Freud), and composers (Philip Glass). Still, because this the closest scholars have come to an arguable historical setting for the origin of

---

[77]   On the nature of monotheism during Akhnaten's reign, see Wente 2000.

Yahwism, the thesis has spawned unabated scholarship.[78] Yet, it is generally conceded that, even if it was a form of monotheism, Atenism was limited both in its time and in its circle of worshipers.

4. Polytheism[79]

These attempts at locating the birth of Yahwism beyond Israel are themselves interesting, for they are driven by the certitude that monotheistic belief is a moral, spiritual, or intellectual advance over polytheism. Belief in a single god may seem obvious to followers of Abrahamic faiths who might even organize missions to spread it; but I doubt that it was deemed so in ancient times and in our own days a good half of humankind is happy to remain polytheistic. In fact, long before we first meet them though written sources, the polytheists of the ancient Near East had abandoned the animism or fetishism historians of religions had predicated for them as first steps in religious illumination. The model that their theologians strove for was essentially humanistic, in that the cosmos was crafted to mirror human sensibilities, with connections between the gods explained in kinship terminology, as mothers, fathers, sisters, and brothers. In this way, the gods were not beyond human comprehension so that entreaties to reach them needed simply to draw on human experience and emotion. Not surprisingly, the prayers and hymns that we have

---

[78] The recent essay of Propp 1999 contains a rich bibliography. See also de Moor, 1990: 71-102; Assmann 1997; Baines 2000 (fine overview). Docker (2001) condemns Freud's thesis on Moses and monotheism for its endorsement of "of one of Christianity's crimes against humanity, its destruction of paganism."

[79] See the good pages of Buccellati 1995 and of Baines 2000, especially pp. 16-22.

from ancient Egypt and Mesopotamia are capable not only of matching the intense piety of our psalmists; but they can also attain an intimacy with the divine that is worthy of our most profound mystics.[80]

For a polytheist, immortal though the gods may be, they too operated under a morally supreme order, which we might call

---

[80] We are still learning much about the gods of the ancient Near East and about their worship. We form our opinions on them from a much broader range of material than is given to us in the Bible. To take Mesopotamia for example, we have the great myths, such as Enuma Elish, and we have sagas of heroes, such as Gilgamesh, in which much information on the gods is embedded. But we also have the incantations of priests, the pious words of kings, the oracles of prophets, the manuals of diviners, the prayers of individuals, and the healing ceremonies of the magicians. Through archaeology, we also have access to temples, decorated with religious scenes and containing religious artifacts. This treasure trove leaves us with no doubts that plurality of gods did not diminish the subtlety, gravity, and intensity of the religious experience the gods evoked in their worshipers. Here is the prayer of a diviner who is seeking to know the will of the gods by reading the omens on the organs of a sacrificed sheep (after Stephens 1969: 391):

They are lying down, the great ones [= the gods].
The bolts are fallen; the fastenings are placed,
The crowds and people are quiet,
The open gates are (now) closed.
The gods of the land and the goddesses of the land,
Shamash, Sin, Adad, and Ishtar,
Have betaken themselves to sleep in heaven.
They are not pronouncing judgments;
They are not deciding things.
Veiled is the night ...
O great ones, gods of the night ...
Stand by, and then,
In the divination which I am making,
In the lamb I am offering,
Put truth to me.

This little text conveys to us a theology that is prevalent in a polytheistic system, where each god may not know the full version of any truth. Notice how the major gods are asleep and that only the great ones, referring to the constellations in heaven, are there to enlighten our diviner.

fate. (Common terms are ME in Sumerian, šimtum in Akkadian, and Maʿat in Egyptian; but there are others.) I cannot say that we fully understand its theological underpinning; but in effect, gods no less than human beings were cogs in a large cosmological wheel, subject to causes and consequences that, albeit pre-destined, were nevertheless within comprehension of gods and mortals.[81] In monotheism, when bad events overtake good believers, the range of explanations is limited, at best to the notion that we are being tested; at worst, that we are paying for our sins. Polytheists, however, did not have to accept blame for faults not felt to be theirs. Rather, they found an explanation in a destiny that was forever choreographing the changing fates of each and all. Since this issue has consequence for our theme, we need to say something about it.

5. The Rise and Fall of the gods

We are discovering that in a polytheistic system gods rise and fall, requiring theological adjustments as explanation. The change of prestige depended on many factors, but invariably it was related to the rise and fall of the city-states in which they are main gods; the parallelism between the human and celestial spheres of activity

---

[81] In contrast, the God of monotheism was always in full control. Yet, because his decisions could be unfathomable, probably under the influence of Persian dualism Judaism gave Satan power over the realm of evil. It is ironic that in Rabbinic Judaism Metatron, a divinized Enoch, is imagined as counterweight to Satan, acting as God's executive; for text and comments, see Alexander 1983; for Metatron, see Halperin 1988: 420-429 Abrams 1994; Idel 1990; for Akatriel, an avatar of Metatron, see Abrams 1996.

being a major component in polytheistic cosmography.[82] The political and martial successes of imperial nations such as Assyria and Babylon can lead to theological refinements in which the main deity is said to rule the other gods, not infrequently absorbing their essence. Such theological cannibalism is manifest in, for example, the famous "Enuma Elish." This Mesopotamian text is rooted deeply in the second millennium BCE. It opens on a *theogony* that focuses primarily on the birth of Marduk and details his preparation for a great *theomachy*, the battle that pits him against Tiamat, a force that represents consciousness without desire, existence without purpose. Victorious, Marduk rules the gods, deploying them into a new cosmic order. His triumph also explains why his city, Babylon, is queen of the world.[83]

---

[82]   Other scenarios include: A city that is poor will worship fewer gods because it lacks the wealth to multiply shrines and so, paradoxically, enhancing their prestige among locales. Or, a conquering city will increase the number of the shrines it supports, making room not just for its own gods, but also for those of conquered powers. Either occasion could inspire adjustment in the kingship among the gods. This explains why scholarly attempts to establish a stable genealogy for the gods can be frustrating.

[83]   "Enuma Elish" is often translated, perhaps most accessibly in Foster 1995: 9-51. Still useful interpretively is Heidel 1951.

  The celestial kingship of deities meant not only that their cities triumphed, but that the earthly kings of such cities became exalted. At their discretion, gods can bestow and withdraw favors, especially to rulers of cities. Occasionally we find a text that tells us why. Around 1770 BCE, the god Adad sends a prophet to deliver a message to king Zimri-Lim of Mari. Here is a paraphrase of what this god had to say:

  I had given all the land [of your kingdom] to your father and, because of my weapons, he had no opponents. But when he abandoned me, I took his land away and gave it to his enemy. But then I restored you to *your father's throne* and handed you the weapons with which I battled the Sea [symbol of chaos]. I rubbed your body with oil from my own numinous glow so that no one could ever stand up to you. Now therefore listen to my only wish: Whenever anyone appeals to you for judgment, saying, "I am aggrieved"; be there to decide his case and to give him satisfaction. This is all that I desire of you. (A. 1968; after Durand 1993: 43-46).

These are noble convictions and the sentiments and metaphors that dispense them must surely transport us to Scripture, for example to 2 Samuel 7: 8-16.

If gods can rise and begin to rule the cosmos, it follows also that other gods must fall or step aside. In Mesopotamian lore, this principle is best displayed in a category of texts we call "city laments."[84] In this genre, permutation of power is conveyed by shift of power among great cities. The poets reflect on these events by describing the horrors that befall a town and its population when the gods, acting in assembly, decide to shift their support elsewhere. The deity of the fallen city begs repeatedly and poignantly for survival or even surcease, but to no avail. Despite the blamelessness of the deity and the innocence of worshipers, the terrible verdict was set. This point is brutally advanced in one lament, when the Moon-god Nanna is told about the fate of his city, Ur:

> The verdict of the assembly cannot be turned back,
>
> The word commanded by [the god] Enlil knows no overturning:
>
> Ur was granted kingship, it was not granted an eternal reign.
>
> Since days of yore when land was founded and people multiplied,
>
> Who has ever witnessed a reign of kingship that has maintained preeminence?
>
> [Ur's] kingship has indeed been long, but is now drained.
>
> O my Nanna, do not exhaust yourself; just leave your city.[85]

---

[84] A good overview of the subject is by Hallo 1995 (bibliography). From Mesopotamia, we have two versions of a lament on the destruction of Sumer and Ur (Klein 1997; Michalowski 1989), and one each of Nippur (Tinney 1996), Eridu (Green 1978) and Uruk (Green 1984). Although they may differ from each other in structure and goals, we can group them within a genre of literature that is written by poets seeking to cajole the gods not to visit the disaster on their own cities.

[85] After Kramer 1969: 617; see also Michalowski 1989: 59, lines 364-370. Dobbs-Alsop (1993, 2000) explores the relationship between the Mesopotamian and biblical displays of the genre.

When hope eventually returns, it is to a diminished Ur, and the lesson that the poet draws for audiences in the new centers of power is about impermanence; for even as they marvel at the tragedy of others, their own cannot be far ahead. Paradoxically, the poet is also comforting, for if gods cannot change fate what is there for humans to do? The observation is worth retaining as we get back to Yahwism and the faith of Israel.

D. THE HEBREW GOD
1. The God of Hebrew Scriptures

Among the Hebrews, as was true all over the Ancient Near East, the presence of God was taken for granted and needed no proof. As the poets of Israel counseled, the whole cosmos attested to God's presence and only fools denied divine existence (Psalm 14). Poets and narrators contributed towards this appreciation for the presence of God in the Hebrew Bible, an encyclopedia on the relationship between God and Israel.[86]

a. The Birth of God

The most striking aspect of God's presence in the Hebrew Bible is that he is given no pre-history and no antecedence. When he first appears in Genesis, the book with which Hebrew editors opened their narrative, no explanation was deemed necessary to slacken our curiosity about his origins. This is noteworthy because,

---

[86] We must not confuse this compilation with expanded editions that included the concept of an international (rather than just a universal) God, the belief in the resurrection of the dead, in heaven and hell, and in an eschatological messianism. All these are developed or refined in the Hellenistic period and after. See below.

as we saw, the explanation of how gods came to be is protean in ancient near eastern lore. In antiquity, speculating about the birth of god was not a sacrilege, for *theogony* was also cosmography, and charting the bloodline of the gods provided a map of the universe, a key to the mystery of creation, and a blueprint for human endeavors.

In contrast, Israel finessed the issue of God's birth by opening its compilation of sacred literature on Genesis 1:1-5. Recall that when God began to create the heavens and the earth (that is the cosmos), earth was mishmash, darkness was over the deep, and a wind from God was sweeping over waters. Not much promise. But out of nothing God created light and, placing it in oscillation with darkness, created "one day," so a basic measure for time. This one day became the building block by which to create the year, the month, and then the week.[87] Because God anteceded time, the Hebrew could argue that no genealogy could be forged for him. Because even gods needed a before and an after (that is, time) when generating each other, the whole issue of God's pedigree, therefore, become moot as far as Israel was concerned. By eschewing any kinship ties for their god, Israel's theologians had thus claimed two essential components of monotheism: the singularity as well as the transcendence of God.[88]

---

[87]   See Sasson 1992, forthcoming².

[88]   The best guess is that this passage was developed just around the Exilic period, so in the 6th century BCE. Not much later, Isaiah quotes God to say, "Before me no god was formed; nor shall there be after me" (43:10-11) and "I am first, I am the last; there is no god besides me" (44:6; see also 45:5-6). But see below.

b. The Birth of Humanity

While they provided no prehistory for their God, the Hebrews presented him as absorbed in the creation and destiny of human beings. It is interesting to note that the Egypt largely ignored the creation of humanity in their mythmaking, while the Mesopotamians broached the topic tangentially or when reaching other objectives.[89] It is not accidental that the Hebrews give names to the first human beings, even if those names initially serve etiological functions: Adam the "Earthling" and Eve, the "Life-force."[90] Human beings, it is explained, are part of an intrinsic scheme, not to labor endlessly for the gods (as is told in Mesopotamia), but to fulfill the spiritual greatness expected of them by one God. Unusual in antiquity, too, is the care with which the Hebrew choreographed a historical moment in which spiritual illumination descended on a childless couple (Abram and Sarai), inspiring them to abandon the familiar for the uncharted. As far as I know, the Romans–perhaps also the Aztecs–excepted, no other people told about beginnings that were initially so unpromising.

2. The Great Hebrew Myth

From Hebrew scripture we are also missing that other great

---

[89] This is true even for Atrahasis, a myth that sought to explain how infertility, miscarriage, child mortality, and birth taboos were divinely ordained to limit an explosion in population explosion that might challenge the gods; see Moran 1970, Frymer-Kensky 1977, and Veenhof 1990. For an overview of Mesopotamian narratives that mention the creation of humanity see Bottéro and Kramer 1989: 502-564.

[90] In the "Creation of Mankind," a text produced in Sumerian and Akkadian, the first human beings are called Ullegarra and Annegarra, names that are unknown from elsewhere; see Bottéro and Kramer 1989: 502-511.

theme in ancient near eastern theology: the great battle that explains how one god rises above the others, as featured in such texts as Enuma Elish where the apotheosis of Marduk is rehearsed. In its best poetry, Scripture does indeed glory in a warrior God who battles Leviathan and Rahab, primordial sea-monsters, Yam and Nahar, the primeval floodgates, Sheol and Mot, symbols of death.[91] Yet, the Hebrew prophets and psalmists called on these Canaanite deities only to forge metaphors and to enrich imagery, much as Venus and Jove served the poets of Christian Europe. The many angels mentioned throughout Scripture as members of a divine council or as soldiers in God's army were never active deities and so never received worship. We can therefore feel certain that, likely long before the end of the Judah's independence, at least one additional element in monotheism, namely the omnipotence of God, had come to be actively promoted.

For the Hebrews, however, God's greatest victories were not cosmic but occurred on earth, God defeats pharaoh's armies (Exodus 15), battles the Amalekites (Exodus 18:16), batters the Amorites with hailstones and, to further their discomfiture, stops the sun in its course (Joshua 10:10-15). God marshals the stars against Sisera (Judges 5:20) and humiliates the prophets of Baal (1 Kings 18:20-40), his numerous deeds in behalf of Israel filling

---

[91] Much has been written on this topic. A recent review of material and opinion is in Day 1985.

a book, now unfortunately lost to us, called "The Wars of the Lord" (Numbers 21:14-15). If we are asked to identify Israel's real myth, it would not be about any cosmic or nature struggle, but that this powerful God, creator of everything that ever was and will be, was devoted almost exclusively, even obsessively, to shaping the future of one people.[92]

E. THE DEMOCRATIZATION OF MONOTHEISM
1. The Promised Land

Indeed, as we saw in the first lecture, the story that Scripture tells really has only two protagonists: God and Israel. The story itself is an optimized and didactic version of the past rather than one we can enter into our history books. Its vision is of a God who from the beginning of time had vowed a land to Israel's ancestors. The land is his and is only leased to those who deserve it. Too often, his chosen people prove themselves unworthy of the promise. Yet, even when he punishes them for abusing his trust by delivering the land to others, his covenant with Israel is eternal.

---

[92] That the Hebrews scrolls (papyrus then leather) had ample opportunity to endlessly replay or deepen this myth (see the First Lecture), could only have sharpened this startling notion; the repeated rephrasing of YHWH's singular absorption with Israel being a major trait for Israel's distinctiveness; see Machinist 1990: 205-207; interesting remarks on this topic in Gnuse 1989. I cannot claim that this conceit was always in Hebrew thought; however, it must have been so when compilers of traditions chose to initiate their story not when Father Abraham walked with God but with divine consecration of the seventh day since creation. In imitation, Israel, alone among the nations on earth, devoted itself to special worship on this seventh day, calling it the "Sabbath." For Israel, it must have seemed especially meaningful that God would have staged the birth of history as omen to the special commitment they would have for each other.

In the Second Lecture, however, we met with a reality of a different sort, a land that was actually controlled by the Hebrews for a relatively brief period. As an independent nation, Israel, in the North, could not have lasted much longer than 250 years. Judah, in the South, lasted a bit longer, perhaps as much as 350 years. These kingdoms were of about the extent of successful dynasties in the ancient Near East; but their duration was not very lengthy when you compare them to the period of rule by dynasties in Egypt, Babylon, Rome, and Byzantium. The Hebrews, too, knew that theirs was but a small sliver of a land where their powerful neighbors often met each other in battle. Periodically, the gods of Israel's enemies would bring formidable armies to Israel and, more often than not, walked away with huge spoils. With a history so full of woes and defeats, with evidence of battle successes for foreign gods, the question for us is, why would Israel place its fate in one God, when that God has not been especially successful against the competing gods? In closing this lecture, I speculate on this issue by focusing specifically on the fate of Jerusalem.

2. Jerusalem

David founded Jerusalem when the Kingdom of Israel was united, let us say around 1000 BCE. But within a generation of the death of his son Solomon, the kingdom split into two parts. The North was called Israel and its capital was Samaria. The south became Judah, with Jerusalem as its capital. If we rely on the archaeological evidence assembled in recent years, two major cataclysms reshaped Jerusalem. The first occurred when the prosperous, religiously cosmopolitan, and politically significant Kingdom of Israel defied the Assyrians. Around 722, the Assyrians swooped down on Samaria, capital of the Northern Kingdom, destroying its major cities and deporting vast numbers to oblivion into the Mesopotamian hinterland, so fostering the myth of the ten lost tribes. In their place, people were brought from as far away as Babylon, taking possession of a number of emptied towns (2 Kings 17:24), among them these transplanted settlers were folks that were later known as Samaritans. Those who remained behind quickly became absorbed in the general population, reverting to a mode of life that was prevalent among Canaanites and Phoenicians.

But a significant group of elite did escape to Judah and settled in Jerusalem. They swelled its modest population; more importantly, they brought with them a strong conviction that their own fate was fully deserved for they had repeatedly angered God (2 Kings 17). Subsequent to the arrival of the refugees, in Jerusalem there came to be a palpable rise in theological fervor, cumulating in a major drive to rid the capital, if not also the countryside, of any traces of pagan worship.[93] With nostalgia, but also much embellishment, the inhabitants recalled the time of David, when Israel and Judah were united. They told of a twofold covenant between God and his people: If Israel obeys the laws of God, God would protect it eternally, his land forever willed to Israel. Moreover, even if its kings sin against God, sovereignty nevertheless would remain attached to the dynasty of David.[94]

---

[93] This observation is widely shared in the literature; see Weinfeld 1991: 50-53.
[94] See Nathan's prophecy, 2 Samuel 7:5-17. On this twofold covenant, see Weinfeld 1970, whose opinion is challenged by Knoppers 1996. See also McKenzie 2001.

This reassurance of stability under God has led some scholars to locate the triumph of monotheism to this period (Halpern 1993); but there are too many contrary testimonies, both textual and archeological, to permit unanimity on this score, such as reports that Judeans were worshiping the Queen of Heaven (Jeremiah 44:24-25) and the discovery of fertility figurines galore. The cautious opinion is that, as Judah was enjoying its last moments of freedom, YHWH had come to be supreme, but not yet unique.

3. Exile and Restoration

The second cataclysm to shape Jerusalem occurred about 150 years after the fall of Samaria. Ignoring the warnings of Jeremiah, Judah challenged Babylon, which brought its armies and leveled Jerusalem, torching Solomon's temple. Archeologists are not in harmony about what happened when Jerusalem fell to the Babylonians and Solomon's temple was leveled.[95] There is evidence that the destruction was selective, mainly around Jerusalem and in foothills, with many regions of Judah left untouched, probably because they submitted to the conquerors. Yet there are also estimates that the population of Judah lost more than half of its total; from 100,000 it shrunk to 40,000. How many of them escaped to Egypt or were taken captives to Babylon is also disputed. The Biblical figures in 2 Kings 24 and in Jeremiah 52 are not easily harmonized and we must just be resigned to not have a clear accounting.[96]

---

[95] An accessible venting of the issues is in a recent issue of the *Biblical Archaeology Review* featuring articles by Blenkinsopp (2002) and Stern (2002).

[96] See Finkelstein 2001: 305-308; Lipschitz (forthcoming).

Scripture, however, tells the same story, but couched more ideologically, hence closer to the truth that needed to be believed. We are told that the Babylonians not only emptied Jerusalem and its temples from their treasures, but that they also dragged into exile the flower of its people, leaving only the poor and destitute (2 Kings 24-25; 2 Chronicles 36; Jeremiah 39-40). Either way, for the first time in nearly a half a millennium, the Hebrews had no land in which they were sovereign.

4. YHWH and the Land

You may recall what I said about the literature of laments by which the fall of powerful states was attributed to a shift in grace from one deity to another. Theologically, the fate of Judah could have had the same explanation: YHWH lost his primacy, and his domain had fallen to the worshipers of Marduk, God of Babylon. Under those circumstances, the promises that YHWH made to his people about land and about sovereignty had to be shelved. Had the survivors of the fall of Jerusalem adopted this way of thinking, they would have accepted their fate as dependent folks. And those exiled in foreign lands would have worshiped the local gods. Something like this had occurred to the people of Samaria. Surprisingly, however, the fate of Samaria was not duplicated in Judah.[97]

---

[97]   On Israelite exiles in Mesopotamia, see Oded 2000.

Less than a half-century later, Babylon's lost heavenly support. Cyrus of Persia entered Babylon on October 12, 539 BCE. The Persians appointed governors with Babylonian names, Sheshbazzar then Zerubbabel, to what was left of Judah, a province now called Yehud whose inhabitants henceforth were Yehûdî, that is "Jews." These governors may or may not have descended from the old royal line; but they were not to rule as kings of a sovereign kingdom. Rather, aided by a modest group of exiled followers but also opposed by the locals, they were to restore order and rebuild a modest version of the temple, just over 70 years after its destruction, so around 515 BCE. In their work, they were helped by the prophets Haggai and Zecharia, who tried to keep the remaining population focused on the old faith, but also shifting divine fulfillment to the end of time. The experiment was not crowned with success, as materially (and likely spiritually) Yehud continued to deteriorate, the victim of political events outside its control.[98] Hope for restored earthly sovereignty was fading.

It is an academic irony (in all of its senses) that a significant theological shift occurred under the sponsorship of two leaders, Ezra and Nehemiah, whose very existence is subject to scholarly debate. We shall not enter this debate, but stay with the accounts that explain how, a half century later, so around 470, with unease about the future, another wave of exiles returned, this time armed with arguments that, in my opinion, reshaped the nature of the Hebrew God.

---

[98] These are nicely described by the Meyers 1993:15-26. See also Lemaire 1996.

Playing like a melody in a Sibelius symphony, fragments of the pre-Exilic theology of God integrated with new themes about that God to deliver the theology of monotheism that is familiar to us. Already before the fall of Judah, YHWH had come to be regarded as unbegotten and likely also unbegetting. Though local, YHWH had been deemed transcendent, perhaps not yet immanent, but also omnipotent, omnipresent, (mostly) omniscient, and universal. But now YHWH was seen also as unique and, equally important, as international.[99] Consequently, no event, political or otherwise, can ever be attributed to a heavenly struggle among the gods, for the simple reason that there are no other gods. Moreover, because YHWH is unique, none of his promises can ever be forfeited. Fulfillment of his commitment to deliver land and sovereignty, therefore, remain potentially at hand. As propounded now, the two components of the argument—the uniqueness of God and the permanence of promise—are mutual and indivisible: Anyone hoping for the end of exile and the restoration of sovereignty must believe in the one God of the unchanging pledge. In this symbiosis of beliefs, there is also an added reciprocity: the longer the promise remains unfulfilled, the heavier becomes the dependence on the uniqueness of God. The deeper is the attachment to one God, the sharper is the conviction about eventual restoration.

So much for the theological argument. And now we come to

---

[99] The portrait was best presented by the prophet (2nd) Isaiah; see 43:10-13, 44:5-8; 45:5-7, 14, 18, 21-22; 46:9. In a vision about the Day of the Lord, that is about the end of times, Zechariah asserts that "The Lord will rule the whole Earth. On that day there will be just one Lord, with just one name" (14:9).

the crucial act that turned an esoteric theological elaboration into a broadly held faith.

5. Public Acceptance

In the book of Ezra, we are given the names of believers who came back with him, and we are told of a regimen of purity that was imposed on all. In Nehemiah (7-8), there is also a report on a remarkable scene that took place in Jerusalem when it remained largely a shambles. We are somewhere around 450 BCE. Gathering as one, the people, native and returning, having prepared themselves with fasting, came to a square at the Temple. With Ezra standing on a dais, the people stood and listened, as far as we knows, to the first public reading of the laws of Moses in Hebrew history.[100] Some scholars are eager to proclaim this moment as the birth of Judaism, because they find it records activities that will later be features of synagogue services. I suggest, however, that this public convocation accomplished much more. In the absence of native rule in Jerusalem and in the uncertainty about religious leadership, the conviction about the unique God and the fulfillment of his promise gained for monotheism organic coherence, constancy, structure, and goal. More importantly, a credo that was held among the elite came to be invested in the multitudes, to have, to hold, and to proclaim wherever they happen to live.

---

[100] Naturally, scholars have differed on the historicity of these proceedings, with some very respected opinions analyzing it as "a free composition" if not a fabrication; see Blenkinsopp 1988: 282-289. The problem is not easily to solve, given the textual untidiness of the material, but we do derive from the passage the notion that the focus of the whole of Israel on the laws of Moses occurred at the conclusion of the exile.

F. CODA

So there we have it: A single god, an eternal promise, a popularized and democratized conviction, a permanence of belief. These components did not come together in 18th Dynasty Egypt or in Imperial Assyria; but they gelled in hapless Yehud, among people who had little to invest except faith and blind hope. There, monotheism took root and became difficult to reverse. I should end here. Yet there must be this coda.

In the centuries since those apprehensive days, when a mutually affirming harmony was achieved between the hope for a restored land and the uniqueness of God, we can say that the idea of monotheism came to a rhetorical and ontological stability. For many Jews and Christians, the establishment of the State of Israel in our days is reward for staying true to the one God and to the promise of restoration. As we know too well, however, this reciprocity of commitments, to the unique god and to the fulfillment of earthly inheritance, has also been the inspiration for immense tragedy, most recently occurring in the modern Near East and now reaching American shores.

Yet, many times during the past centuries that harsh political realities stimulated other perceptions, of God and of his commitment, for alteration in one component necessarily leads to adaptation in the other. Thus, under the influence of Persian dualism, the God of the true promise was matched to a baneful Satan, setting up eschatological battles between Good and Evil. In such a vision, Jerusalem evolved into the center of a heavenly kingdom, rather than one on earth. We all know how this new perception of the promised inheritance allowed some Jews of the Roman period to have a different notion of God, one in which he could beget a son who, through death and resurrection, redeems the faithful into eternal salvation.

But this constant balance between the single god and the singular promise has continued to shape the development of monotheistic faiths. I need not tell you about the Puritans in the New Zion, about the Mormons in Utah, the Dutch in South Africa, and the Protestants in Northern Ireland. But in Judaism itself, a major replay of these components occurred during the Middle Ages. At that time, living in an increasingly inhospitable Europe, with Jerusalem beyond their reach, and God seemingly too remote, Jewish sages radically reconfigured God as well as the promise. In the Zohar, the famous anchor for the Kabbalah, they carved the body of God into 10 spiritual manifestations. Each of these manifestations had its concrete, earthly mirror, with each realm having the potential to reshape the other. The bridge for mutual harmony between and among the parts was to be the work of the *tsadiqim*, righteous mystics who discovered the way to erase the boundary between heaven and earth, the human and the divine. [101] This particular movement had a spectacular collapse in the mid-seventeenth century CE, with the failed messianism of Shabbetay Zevi. Yet, since then, this failure has only invited other configurations, among them those of Frankists, Hassids, Zionists, and Schneersonians, all of them meant to keep the believer fixed on the promise, earthly or heavenly, that a unique God is bound to deliver.

---

[101] See A. Green 1977. Fine 1995 is a fine collection of essays on the kabbalah.

A Response to Lecture Three

Fook-Kong WONG

B. Th. (Singapore Bible College), M.T.S., Th. D. (Harvard Divinity School, U.S.A.)

Assistant Professor, Hong Kong Baptist Theological Seminary, Hong Kong

ON THE ORIGINS OF THE HEBREW GOD
And of the Hebrew Faith in God
A Response
Fook Kong Wong

I wish to begin my response by thanking Professor Sasson for an informative and interesting talk. In this third lecture of his series on "Hebrew Origins," he concentrated on the Hebrew religion. He posed three interrelated questions at the beginning of the discourse and answered them in the course of his lecture. I will first review these three questions and the answers that he gave. Then I will comment on some of the pertinent points that he made to each of his questions. Finally, I will spend some time reflecting theologically on the historical-critical approach.

Origins of the Hebrew God

The first question raised by Sasson was, "What do scholars have to say about the origin of the Hebrew God, especially in comparison with what we have learned about the gods of the ancient Near East?" The answer to this question is that "as yet we have not located reliable testimony to establish who first worshiped YHWH and where" (p. 79). Furthermore, "how the Hebrews came to YHWH as the sponsor of their destiny remains a question for the philosopher and the theologian rather than the historian and philologist" (p. 79). To state the answer in another way, we do not know if the Hebrews adopted the worship of YHWH from another group of people or that it originated from them. Moreover, we also do not know the circumstance that led to the Hebrews' adoption of YHWH as their God.

Response : Fook Kong Wong

This is a fair assessment of the state of historical-critical scholarship on this topic. It does not mean that we do not know what the Bible says about these issues. It simply means that we do not have sufficient data outside of the Bible to ascertain the authenticity of its account. As far as the Bible is concerned, most of the important personalities in Genesis leading up to Moses knew YHWH by name.[1] This includes Eve (4:1), Lamech (5:29), Noah (9:26), Abraham (13:4; 15:2), Hagar (16:13), Isaac (25:21; 26:25), Jacob (28:13, 16), and Rachel (30:24). There is a reference in Genesis 4:26 about humans beginning to worship YHWH during the time of Seth, the son of Adam and Eve. There is also a reference to a group of people using the expression "like Nimrod, a mighty hunter before YHWH" (10:9). Thus as far as the Bible is concerned, the first humans knew God by his name. Many people, known and unknown to us from the Bible, also apparently knew God by name. When YHWH announced his name to Moses, it was not the first time he made himself known to humankind by name.[2]

What we do find from archaeology regarding the worship of YHWH in ancient Israel was that it was syncretistic in nature. To

---

[1] For our purpose there is no need to identify the sources of the biblical texts. In the classical formulation of the Documentary Hypothesis all the texts quoted below are from the J source [See Martin Noth, *A History of Pentateuchal Traditions*, translated by B.W. Anderson (Chico, Calif.: Scholar Press, 1981), 262–267.] The Documentary Hypothesis has been challenged and modified innumerable ways. For a short but informative summary of the trends see J. Blenkinsopp, "The Pentateuch," in John Barton, ed., *The Cambridge Companion to Biblical Interpretation*, (Cambridge: Cambridge University Press, 1998), 181–197.

[2] For a good summary of the views on the name of God see G. J. Botterweck and H. Ringgren (eds.), translated by D. E. Green, *Theological Dictionary of the Old Testament*, vol. 5 (Grand Rapids, Mich.: Eerdmans, 1986), 500–521.

elaborate more on the example from Kuntillet ʿAdjrud that J. Sasson mentioned, this small site is about 50 km south of Kadesh-Barnea. It is dated from between the mid-9th to the mid-8th century BCE based on pottery types (common in both Judah and Israel)[3] or the beginning of the 8th century BCE (the reign of Jehoash) based on paleography and internal analysis of the texts.[4] Heterodoxy is indicated at this site from the following facts. First, names like "YHWH of Samaria," and "YHWH of Teman." This way of naming the gods is well attested in non-Israelites divine names (e.g., Hadad of Sikan, Asherah of Tyre, Ashtart of Kition). A variation of this type of names is the Tannit-in-Lebanon or Ashtart-in-Sidon type.[5] This variation is also found in the Bible. Examples include YHWH-in-Hebron (2 Sam. 15:7), Ps 99:2 (YHWH in Zion) and Dagon-in-Ashdod (1 Sam. 5:5). These examples show that there were Israelites who identified YHWH with towns or cities just as was done among their neighbors. Second, the name YHWH is followed in every instance by, "and to/by his/its Asherah." Asherah was a goddess in the pantheon of Canaan. A basic rule of Hebrew grammar is that proper noun does not take a suffix. Therefore, scholars have disagreed on whether the word referred to the goddess Asherah or to a cultic object of YHWH at ʿAdjrud. Regardless of which explanation is right, we are still dealing with a type of religious practice that is condemned in our Hebrew Bible.

---

[3]   Amihai Mazar, *Archaeology of the Land of the Bible* (New York: Doubleday, 1990), 449.

[4]   P. Kyle McCarter, Jr., "Aspects of the Religion of the Israelite Monarchy: Biblical and Epigraphic Data," in P. D. Miller, Jr., P. D. Hanson, and S. D. McBride, eds., *Ancient Israelite Religion: Essays in Honor of Frank Moore Cross* (Philadelphia: Fortress Press, 1987), 138.

[5]   Ibid, 140–141.

Response :   Fook Kong Wong

Distinctive Characteristics of Israel's Faith

The second question that Sasson raised was, "What was distinctive in Israel's worship of that God?" In answer to this question, he listed six distinctive characteristics of Israel's worship of YHWH: a) Observance of Sabbath, b) circumcision of male babies on the second week after their birth, c) relentless codification of food and purity taboos, d) regulation of even personal aspects of the believer's life, e) denying its women direct access to God, and, f) monotheism (p. 92). Apart from monotheism, the others were listed without further discussion. I have nothing much to add to what he has said.

Nature of Israel's Monotheistic Faith

The last characteristic listed by Sasson occupied the final section of his lecture and answers his third question, "What can we say about the idea of a unique God?" The ensuing discussion of Israel's monotheistic faith occupies more than half of the lecture and is, therefore, an important part of his topic on Israel's religion. In this section, Sasson looked at other monotheistic faiths in the ancient Near East as well as the nature of polytheistic faiths in these cultures. He then went on to contrast the conception of God found in the Hebrew Bible and the ancient Near East. According to Sasson, "The most striking aspect of God's presence in the Hebrew Bible is that he is given no pre-history and no antecedence" (page 104). Thus the singularity and transcendence of God is emphasized. Furthermore, there is no story about YHWH's battle with other gods for supremacy. Sasson thinks that monotheism triumphed over polytheism only in the post-exilic period. The exiles adopted a strict monotheistic faith to comfort themselves that YHWH has not been displaced by other gods. Obviously if there is only one God, he cannot be dethroned by another god. Therefore, YHWH could still fulfill his promise to give the land back to them.

I agree with the broad outline of ancient Israelite religion that he has sketched. I wish to add that what we can gather from the Bible regarding Israel's monotheistic faith probably represented a subset of the wider phenomenon. According to Michael D. Coogan, "it is essential to consider biblical religion as a subset of Israelite religion and Israelite religion as a subset of Canaanite religion."[6] One can compare ancient Israelite religion to what is commonly called "Biblical Hebrew" or "Classical Hebrew." Hebrew was a living language that continued to change and develop over a period of time. Furthermore there were at least two dialects of Hebrew (northern and southern) in the pre-exilic period itself. Therefore, what we have in our Hebrew Bible is an anthology of Hebrew dialects over a period of time. What we call "Biblical Hebrew" is really the majority Hebrew represented in the Hebrew Bible.[7] The same can be said of the study of ancient Israelite religion. Israel's religious life was a multi-faceted phenomenon that evolved over a period of time, sometimes differently in different places and among different strata of society.

---

[6] "Canaanite Origin and Lineage: Reflections on the Religion of Ancient Israel," in P. D. Miller, Jr., P. D. Hanson, and S. D. McBride, eds., *Ancient Israelite Religion: Essays in Honor of Frank Moore Cross* (Philadelphia: Fortress Press, 1987), 115.

[7] See, for example, Bruce K. Waltke, and M. O'Connor, *An Introduction to Biblical Syntax* (Winona Lake, Ind.: Eisenbrauns, 1990), 3–43.

Furthermore, I think that any statement about the triumph of monotheism in the post-exilic period should be done with caution. We arrive at this conclusion mainly from texts of the period that espoused philosophical monotheism (e.g., Isaiah 43: 10–13; 45: 5–7) as well as the religious stance of some of the leaders (e.g. Ezra, Nehemiah). However this might not have been the theology of the masses. It is a truism to say that the religion of the great theologians of any religion may not reflect the religious beliefs of the man on the street. There is a difference between the formal or institutional expression of a religion and the local expressions of the same religion at the grass root level.[8] From pre-exilic period, this point is amply illustrated by the syncretistic form of religion adopted by the people at Kuntillet ʿAdjrud in contrast to the strict form of religion advocated by the prophets. I suspect that the situation was not too different in the post-exilic period. The books of Ezra (chapters 9–10) and Nehemiah (10: 28–39; 12: 4–31) give us a glimpse of religious life in the post-exilic period in Yehud and they paint a picture of a community struggling with religious purity and fervor.

When we turn to the books of 1 and 2 Chronicles, a post-exilic work, we find evidences of heterodoxy that are similar to those that we found in pre-exilic Israel. 1 Chronicles 16: 25–26 say, "For great is YHWH and greatly to be praised, he is to be feared

---

8   See Paul G. Hiebert, R. Daniel Shaw, and Tite Tienou, *Understanding Folk Religion: A Christian Response to Popular Beliefs and Practices* (Grand Rapids, Mich.: Baker Books, 1999), 73–92, for a discussion of the differences between the institutional form of a religion and the form of the religion at the grass root, i.e., folk, level.

above all gods; For all the gods of the peoples are idols, but YHWH made the heavens."[9] The word for "idols" (Mylyl)) could also mean "non-existence."[10] On the surface this seems like an example of monotheistic theology. However, why would YHWH be compared to non-existent entities? Also, the phrase "he is to be feared above all gods" presumes that the other gods should be feared too, although less than YHWH.[11] Therefore, what we have in this verse is something less than strict monotheism. Even more telling are the comparisons between YHWH and other gods in 2 Chronicles 2: 4 ("And the house which I am about to build will be great, for greater is our God than all the gods")[12] and 6: 14 ("O YHWH, the God of Israel, there is no god like you in heaven or on earth ...").[13] For these reasons, I am more inclined to think that monotheism enjoyed a revival in the post-exilic period rather than to think that it achieved some sort of hegemony over the religious thought of the people.

Finally, J. Sasson's suggestion that "the conviction about the unique God and the fulfillment of his promise gained for monotheism organic coherence, constancy, structure, and goal," (page 111) is a legitimate point. I have no problem believing that a group of people threatened on all sides would choose a stricter version of their faith to help them face a hostile world. I want to

---

[9] Identical to Ps.96:4–5.
[10] L. Koehler and W. Baumgartner, edited by M. E. J. Richardson, *The Hebrew and Aramaic Lexicon of the Old Testament*, vol. 1 (Leiden: E. J. Brill, 1994), 56.
[11] See discussion by Sara Japhet, *The Ideology of the Book of Chronicles and Its Place in Biblical Thought* (New York: Peter Lang, 1989), 41–53.
[12] 2: 5 in the English translation.
[13] Identical to 1 Kings 8:23.

add another suggestion to his point. From the books of Ezra and Nehemiah we find that the returnees were more religiously committed than the inhabitants of Jerusalem and the surrounding areas. There might have been many reasons for this state of affair. I think a major factor was the need for ethnic boundary.[14] The question of what defined them as a people must have concerned them just as it concerns their descendents up to the present.[15] Celebration of the Sabbath and other festivals, circumcision, dietary laws, and monotheism were some of the things they chose to distinguish themselves from their neighbors. I do not mean that these practices originated in the post-exilic period. What I mean is that the exiles found that they alone among their neighbors observed some of these practices and that they alone had a strong monotheistic component to their religion. Thus these practices were emphasized. In addition, they rejected polytheism because their captors and neighbors were polytheistic. Those who were left behind in Judah, on the other hand, did not have the same need to distinguish themselves. They were still the "People of the Land." As a result, the returnees were stricter in their beliefs and practices than the inhabitants of Jerusalem and the surrounding regions.

---

[14] For a discussion of the issue of ethnicity in the exilic period, see Kenton L. Sparks, *Ethnicity and Identity in Ancient Israel: Prolegomena to the Study of Ethnic Sentiments and Their Expression in the Hebrew Bible* (Winona Lake, Ind.: Eisenbrauns, 1998), 285–319.

[15] This concern can be seen in the multitude of books on what it means to be a Jew. See, for example, Shaye J. D. Cohen, *The Beginnings of Jewishness: Boundaries, Varieties, Uncertainties* (Berkeley: University of California Press, 1999); Walter Homolka, Walter Jacob, Esther Seidel, eds., *Not by Birth Alone: Conversion to Judaism* (London & Washington [D. C.]: Cassell, 1997).

Theological Reflection on Historical Criticism

In closing, I want to spend some time reflecting on historical criticism. Perhaps some people are disturbed by the conclusions reached in this series of lectures. In his stimulating article, "The Hebrew Bible, the Old Testament, and Historical Criticism," Jon Levenson compared historical criticism to psychoanalysis.

> It brings to light what has been repressed and even forgotten, the childhood, as it were, of the tradition. But if Wordsworth was right that 'the Child is the Father of the Man,' it is wrong to think that the man will be happy to meet the child within him whom he thinks he has outgrown. Like psychoanalysis, historical criticism uncovers old conflicts and dissolves the impression that they have been resolved rather than repressed.[16]

Ancient Israelite religion being the "Child" that is the "Father" of Christianity, any digging into its history is bound to be a nerve wrecking, and perhaps painful, experience for most Christians. I imagine the same would be true of my Jewish friends.

---

[16] Jon Levenson, *Jews and Christians in Biblical Studies: The Hebrew Bible, the Old Testament, and Historical Criticism* (Louisville, Ky.: Westminster/John Knox Press, 1993), 4.

Response : Fook Kong Wong

When we look into the dim historical past, we find that what we have might not have been the "real" past, but only a re-telling of the past that was shaped by theological concerns. Similarly, what we have might not have been the revelation at Mt. Sinai as much as interpretation/s of the revelation. Also, the understanding of God as we have it today (e.g., unique, eternal, universal, omnipotent, omniscience) was not reached until the exilic period. How are we to digest these conclusions theologically? To put it differently, if God really appeared to Israel at Mt. Sinai, why did they not arrive at our understanding of God until so late?

First, we can draw an analogy between God's dealing with Israel and his dealing with us. We know enough about God at a certain point in time to believe in him. This point is the beginning of our faith journey. We spend the rest of our lives learning more and more about him. Similarly, the patriarchs' understanding of God probably evolved over a period of time. Furthermore, Israel was not given a set of doctrines regarding God at Mt. Sinai. Rather they were given a covenant and its stipulations. We have to presume that they had different views concerning that revelation then and later. Therefore, we should not be surprised that some of these transitory views are preserved in the Bible.

This brings me to the second point. As Christians, our conception of God should not be derived from any sect or any period of Israel's history. In fact, it should not even be derived from the Hebrew Bible alone. Rather, it should be derived from the Christian canon. As B. Childs already insisted a few decades ago, "The significance of the final form of the biblical text is that it alone bears witness to the full history of revelation."[17] Whether we realize it or not we are already reading the OT in light of the NT. For example, we interpret Is. 7:14 in light of Matt. 1:15–18 (esp. vv. 23, 25). Similarly, we identify the Suffering Servant in Is. 53 with Jesus because that is how he is understood in the gospels (e.g., v. 1 cf. Jn. 12: 38; v. 4 cf. Matt. 8:17). We read the Bible this way because we believe that the final and most perfect revelation of God is in Christ (Heb. 1: 1–2; John 1: 1–5, 9–18). When we work from such a theological perspective, studying the Bible from a historical-critical approach is less painful and it may yield important insights into God's Word.

---

[17]   *Introduction to the Old Testament as Scripture* (Philadelphia: Fortress Press, 1979), 76.

Afterword

We have covered much ground in these three lectures and yet many issues were hardly resolved and many subjects were left untouched. But you must recognize by now that, despite its many detours, the stories I have detailed for you on the reconstruction of the Hebrew past as well as on the search for the Hebrew God cannot have finality or ending; for it is the nature of biblical scholarship that each generation of researchers imagines itself better suited than the last, to tackle the problems posed by the Hebrew text, to flesh out Hebraic history, and to establish to origins of Hebrew faith.

My own effort in the above pages was inspired not by the failure of my predecessors–for each and all have bequeathed us precious insights–but by consequences as set for us in the familiar Hebrew parable of the Tower of Babel (Genesis 11:1-9). We are told there that when humanity became wary of a God who could unleash a murderous Flood against it, people caucused and said, "Let us build for ourselves a towering city, its pinnacle in heaven. We shall thereby perpetuate our name, lest we be scattered all over earth." These people failed in their endeavor, of course, because God confused their tongues. What we must understand, too, is that he actually multiplied their interpretive tools, and so guaranteed that their descendants–historians, theologians, philosophers, archeologists, and, for better or worse, political leaders–can never resist searching for solutions to issues raised in the sacred writings of the Hebrews, a people of lesser numbers or power that nonetheless has survived the centuries better than any of its more mighty contemporaries.

Jack M. Sasson

BIBLIOGRAPHY

Abrams, Daniel,

1994:   "The Boundaries of Divine Ontology: The Inclusion and Exclusion of Metatron in the Godhead," *Harvard Theological Review* 87: 291-321.

1996:   "From Divine Shape to Angelic Being: The Career of Akatriel in Jewish Literature," *Journal of Religion* 76: 43-63.

Albright, William F.,

1968:   *Yahweh and the Gods of Canaan. A Historical Analysis of Two Contrasting Faiths* (Jordan Lectures 1965; London: The Athlone Press).

Alexander, P.,

1983:   "3 (Hebrew Apocalypse of) Enoch," pp. 223-315 in James H. Charlesworth (ed), *The Old Testament Pseudepigrapha, volume 1: Apocalyptic Literature and Testaments* (Garden City, N. Y.: Doubleday).

Allam, S.,

2000:   "Slaves," *Oxford Encyclopedia of Ancient Egypt* (New York: Oxford University Press) 3: 293-296.

Assmann, Jan

1998:   *Moses the Egyptian: The Memory of Egypt in Western Monotheism* (Cambridge: Harvard University Press).

Astour, Michael C.,

1959: "Benê-lamina et Jéricho," *Semitica* 9:5-20.

1978: *The Rabbeans: A Tribal Society on the Euphrates from Yahdun-Lim to Julius Caesar* (Syro-Mesopotamian Studies, 2/1; Malibu, Calif.: Undena Publications).

1979: "Yahwe in Egyptian Topographic Lists," pp. 17-34 in Manfred Görg and Edgar Pusch (eds), *Festschrift Elmar Edel, 12 März, 1979. Studien zu Geschichte, Kultur und Religion Ägyptens und des alten Testament, I* (Bamberg: M. Görg).

1999: "The Hapiru in the Amarna Texts. Basic Points of Controversy," *Ugarit-Forschungen* 31: 31-50.

Auld, Graeme,

2000: "Samuel and Genesis: Some Questions of John Van Seters's 'Yahwist'," pp. 23-32 in S. L. McKenzie and Th. Römer (eds) *Rethinking the Foundations: Historiography in the Ancient World and in the Bible. Essays in Honour of John Van Seters.* (Beihefte zur *Zeitschrift für die alttestamentliche Wissenschaft*, 294; Berlin: Walther de Gruyter).

Baines, John,

2000: "Egyptian Deities in Context: Multiplicity, Unity, and the Problem of Change," pp. 9-78 in Porter 2000.

Barré, Michael L.,

1997:   "The Portrait of Balaam in Numbers 22-24," *Interpretation* 51: 254-266.

Barstad, Hans M.,

1996:   *The Myth of the Empty Land: A Study in the History and Archaeology of Judah During the "Exilic" Period* (Symbolae Osloenses, Fasciculi suppletorii, 28; Oslo: Scandinavian University Press).

Biggs, Robert D.,

1992:   "Ebla Texts," *Anchor Bible Dictionary* (New York: Doubleday) 2: 263-270.

Black, J. A. and W. J. Tait,

1995:   "Archives and Libraries in the Ancient Near East," pp. 2197-2209 in Sasson 1995.

Blenkinsopp, Joseph,

2002:   "The Babylonian Gap Revisited: There Was no Gap," *Biblical Archeology Review* 28/3: 36-38, 59.

Bord, Lucien-Jean and David Hamidović,

2002:   "Écoute Israël (Deut. VI 4)," *Vetus Testamentum* 52: 13-29.

Bottéro, Jean and Samuel Noah Kramer

1989:   *Lorsque les dieux faisaient l'homme: Mythologie mésopotamienne* (Paris: Gallimard).

Buccellati, Giorgio
1995:   "Ethics and Piety in the Ancient Near East," pp. 1685-86 in Sasson 1995.

Carroll, Robert P.,
1992:   "The Myth of the Empty Land," *Semeia* 59: 79-93.

Clements, R. E.,
1983:   *A Century of Old Testament Studies* (Guildford: Lutterworth).

Cohen, Shaye J. D.,
1987:   *From the Maccabees to the Mishnah* (Library of Early Christianity; Philadelphia: Westminster Press).

Cogan, Mordecai,
1992:   "Chronology (Hebrew Bible)," *Anchor Bible Dictionary* (New York: Doubleday) 1: 1002-1011.

Cross, Frank M.,
1973:   *Canaanite Myth and Hebrew Epic. Essays in the History of the Religion of Israel* (Cambridge: Harvard University Press).

Cryer, Frederick H.,
1987:   "To the One of Fictive Music: OT Chronology and History," *Scandinavian Journal of the Old Testament* 2: 1-27.

Daniels, Peter T.,

1995:   "The Decipherment of Ancient Near Eastern
            Scripts," pp. 81-93 in Sasson 1995.

Day, John,

1985:   *God's Conflict with the Dragon and the Sea*
            (Cambridge: Cambridge University Press).

1994:   "Yahweh and Gods and Goddesses of Canaan,"
            pp. 181-196 in Dietrich and Klopfenstein 1994.

Dearman, J. Andrew and Gerald L. Mattingly,

1992:   "Mesha Stele," *Anchor Bible Dictionary* (New York:
            Doubleday) 4:708-709.

Demsky, Aaron,

1995:   "On Reading Ancient Inscriptions: The
            Monumental Aramaic Stele Fragment from Tel
            Dan," *Journal of the Ancient Near Eastern Society
            of Columbia University* 23: 29-35.

Dever, William G.,

1994:   "Ancient Israelite Religion: How to Reconcile the
            Differing Textual and Artifactual Portraits?," pp.
            105-125 in Dietrich and Klopfenstein 1994.

2001:   *What did the Biblical Writers Know, and When
            Did they Know it?* (Grand Rapids, Mich.:
            Eerdmans).

Dietrich, Walter and A. Klopfenstein (eds),

1994:   *Ein Gott allein?: YHWH-Verehrung und biblischer Monotheismus im Kontext der Israelitischen und altorientalischen Religionsgeschichte* (Orbis biblicus et orientalis, 139; Göttingen: Vandenhoeck und Ruprecht).

Dobbs-Alsop, F. W.,

1993:   *Weep, O Daughter of Zion: A Study of the City-Lament Genre in the Hebrew Bible* (Biblica et Orientalia, 44; Rome: Pontifical Biblical Institute).

2000:   "Darwinism, Genre Theory, and City Laments," *Journal of the American Oriental Society* 120: 625-630.

Docker, John,

2001:   "In Praise of Polytheism," pp. 140-172 in Roland Boer and Gerald West (eds), *A Vanishing Mediator? The Presence/Absence of the Bible in Postcolonialism* (*Semeia*, 88: Atlanta: Society of Biblical Literature).

Drury, J. (ed),

1989:   *Critics of the Bible 1724-1873* (Cambridge: Cambridge University Press).

Durand, Jean-Marie,

1993:   "Le mythologème du combat entre le dieu de
             l'orage et la mer en Mésopotamie," *MARI.*
             Annales de Recherches Interdisciplinaires 7: 41-
             61.

1992:   "Mari, Texts," *Anchor Bible Dictionary* (New York:
             Doubleday) 4: 529-536.

Emerton, J. A.,

1982:   "New Light on Israelite Religion. The Implication
             of the Inscriptions from Kuntillet ʿajrud," *Zeitschrift*
             für die alttestamentliche Wissenschaft 94: 2-20.

Fine, Lawrence,

1995:   *Essential Papers on Kabbalah* (New York: New York
             University Press, 1995).

Finet, André,

1993:   "Yahvé au royaume de Mari," pp. 15-22 Gyselen,
             Rika (ed), *Circulation des monnaies, des*
             marchandises et des biens (Res orientales 5;
             Leuven: Peeters).

Finkelstein, Israel,

1999:   "State Formation in Israel and Judah: A Contrast
             in Context, A Contrast in Trajectory," *Near Eastern*
             Archaeology 62: 35-52.

Finkelstein, Israel and Neil A. Silberman,

2001:   *The Bible Unearthed. Archeology's New Vision of Ancient Israel and the Origins of Its Sacred texts* (New York: Free Press).

Fiorenza, Elisabeth S.,

1992:   "Feminist Hermeneutics," *Anchor Bible Dictionary* (New York: Doubleday) 2: 783-791.

Fleming, Daniel,

1995:   "More Help from Syria: Introducing Emar to Biblical Study," *Biblical Archaeologist* 58: 139-147.

1998:   "Mari and the Possibilities of Biblical Memory," *Revue d'Assyriologie* 92: 41-78.

Foster, Benjamin R.,

1995:   *From Distant Days. Myths, Tales, and Poetry of Ancient Mesopotamia* (Bethesda, Md.: CDL Press).

Freedman, David Noel, and Michael O'Connor,

1960:   "The Name of the God of Moses," *Journal of Biblical Literature* 79: 151-156.

1980:   "YHWH," *Theological Dictionary of the Old Testament* 5: 500-521.

1987:   "Yahweh of Samaria and His Asherah," *Biblical Archaeologist* 50: 241-249.

Frymer-Kensky, Tikva,

1977:   "The Atrahasis Epic and Its Significance for Our Understanding of Genesis 1-9," *Biblical Archaeologist* 40: 147-155.

Geller, Stephen A.,

2000:   "The God of the Covenant," pp. 273-319 in Porter 2000.

Goetschel, R.,

1987:   "'*Ehyeh Asher Ehey*,' in the Works of the Gerona Kabbalists," pp. 287-298 in J. Dan (ed), *The Beginnings of Jewish Mysticism in Medieval Europe* (Jerusalem Studies in Jewish Thought, 6/3-4; Jerusalem: Department of Jewish Thought). [In Hebrew.]

Goldwasser, Orly,

2001:   "Hieroglyphics," pp. 198-204 in Donald B. Redford (ed), *The Oxford Encyclopedia of Ancient Egypt* (New York: Oxford University Press).

Goodman, Lenn Evan,

1996:   *God of Abraham* (New York: Oxford University Press, 1996).

Gottwald, Norman,
1976:   "War, Holy," pp. 942-944 in K. Crim (ed), *The Interpreter's Dictionary of the Bible. An Illustrated Encyclopedia, Supplementary Volume* (Nashville: Abingdon).

Green, Arthur,
1977:   "*The Zaddiq* as *Axis Mundi* in Later Judaism," *Journal of the American Academy of Religion* 45: 327-347. [Reprinted in Fine 1995: 291-314.]

Green, Margaret W.,
1978:   "The Eridu Lament," *Journal of Cuneiform Studies* 30: 127-167.
1984:   "The Uruk Lament," *Journal of the American Oriental Society* 104:253-279.

Greenspahn, Frederick E.,
1991:   *Essential Papers on Israel and the Ancient Near East* (New York: New York University Press, 1991.

Greenstein, Edward L.,
1990:   "The Formation of the Biblical Narrative Corpus," *Association of Jewish Studies Review* 15: 151-178.

Gnuse, Robert Karl,
1989:   *Heilsgeschichte as a Model for Biblical Theology: The Debate Concerning the Uniqueness and Significance of Israel's Worldview* (Lanham, Md.: University Press of America).

1997:   *No Other Gods : Emergent Monotheism in Israel*
                 (Journal for the Study of the Old Testament:
                 Supplement Series, 241: Sheffield: Sheffield
                 Academic Press).

Hackett, Jo Ann,
1986:   "Some Observations on the Balaam Tradition at
                 Deir ʿAlla," *Biblical Archeologist* 49: 216-222.
1984:   *The Balaam Text from Deir ʿAlla* (Harvard Semitic
                 Monographs, 31; Chico: Scholars Press).

Hadley, J. M.,
1987:   "The Khirbet el-Qom Inscription," *Vetus
                 Testamentum* 37: 50-62.
1994:   "Yahweh and His 'Asherah': Archaeological and
                 Textual Evidence for the Cult of the Goddess," pp.
                 235-268 in Dietrich and Klopfenstein 1994.
2000:   *The Cult of Asherah in Ancient Israel and Judah:
                 Evidence for a Hebrew Goddess* (Cambridge:
                 Cambridge University Press).

Hallo, William W.,
1995:   "Lamentations and Prayers in Sumer and Akkad,"
                 pp. 1871-118 in Sasson 1995.

Hallo, William W. and K. Lawson Younger, Jr.,
2000:   *Context of Scripture, v. 2: Monumental
                 Inscriptions from the Biblical World* (Leiden: Brill).

Halperin, David J.,

1988:   *The Faces of the Chariot* (Texte und Studien zum antiken Judentum, 16: Tübingen: J. C. B. Mohr).

Halpern, Baruch

1992:   "Kenites," *Anchor Bible Dictionary* (New York: Doubleday) 4: 17-22.

1993:   "Monotheism," pp. 524-525 in Bruce M. Metzger and Michael D. Coogan (eds), *The Oxford Companion to the Bible* (New York: Oxford University Press).

Hayes, John H.,

1979:   *An Introduction to Old Testament Study* (Nashville: Abingdon).

Heidel, Alexander,

1951:   *The Babylonian Genesis. The Story of Creation* (second edition; Chicago: University of Chicago Press).

Ho, Craig, Y.S.,

1999:   "The Stories of the Family Troubles of Judah and David: A Study of Their Literary Links," *Vetus Testamentum* 49: 514-531.

Bibliography

Hughes, Jeremy,

1990:   *Secrets of the Times. Myth and History in Biblical Chronology* (Journal for the Study of the Old Testament: Supplement Series, 66; Sheffield: JSOT Press).

Idel, Moshe,

1990:   "Enoch Is Metatron," *Immanuel* 24/25: 220-240.

Keel, Othmar (ed),

1980:   *Monotheismus im alten Israel und seiner Umwelt* (Fribourg: Schweizerisches Katholisches Bibelwerk).

Klein, Jacob

1997:   "Lamentation over the Destruction of Sumer and Ur," pp. 535-539 in William W. Hallo and K. Lawson Younger, Jr. (eds), *Context of Scripture. Volume I: Canonical Compositions from the Biblical World* (Leiden: Brill).

Knauf, Ernst Axel,

1984:   "Yahwe," *Vetus Testamentum* 34: 467-472

1990:   "War 'Biblisch-Hebräisch' eine Sprache?," *Zeitschrift für Althebräistik* 3: 11-23.

Knoppers, Gary N.

1996:   "Ancient Near Eastern Royal Grants and the Davidic Covenant: A Parallel?," *Journal of the American Oriental Society* 116: 670-697.

Lambert, Wilfred G.,

1971: "Gott: Nach akkadischen Texten," *Reallexikon der Assyriologie* 3: 543-546.

1975: "The Historical Development of the Mesopotamian Pantheon: A Study in Sophisticated Polytheism," pp. 191-200 in Hans Goedicke and J. J. M. Roberts (eds), *Unity and Diversity: Essays in History, Literature, and Religion of the Ancient Near East* (Baltimore: The Johns Hopkins University Press).

Lemaire, A.

1977: "Les inscriptions de Khirbet el-Qôm et l'Ashérah de Yhwh," *Revue biblique* 84: 595-608.

1992a: "Ostraca, Semitic," *Anchor Bible Dictionary* (New York: Doubleday) 5: 50-51.

1992b: "Writing and Writing Materials," *Anchor Bible Dictionary* (New York: Doubleday) 6: 999-1008.

1994: "House of David Restored in Moabite Inscription," *Biblical Archaeology Review* 20: 31-37.

1996: "Zorobabel et la Judée à la lumière de l'épigraphie (fin du VIe S. av. J.-C.)," *Revue biblique* 103: 48-57.

1998: "The Tel Dan Inscription Stela as a Piece of Royal Historiography," *Journal for the Study of the Old Testament* 81: 3-14.

Lemche, Niels Peter,

1992: "Ḥabiru, Ḥapiru," *Anchor Bible Dictionary* (New York: Doubleday) 3: 6-10.

L'Heureux, Conrad E.,

1981:   "Searching for the Origins of God," pp. 33-57 in B. Halpern and J. D. Levenson (eds), *Traditions in Transformation. Turning Points in Biblical Faith* (Winona Lake, Ind.: Eisenbrauns).

Lipschitz, Oded,

Forthcoming: "Demographic Changes in Judah between the 7th and 5th Centuries BCE."

Lohfink, Norbert,

1997:   "ḥāram; ḥērem," pp. 180-199 in G. Johannes Botterweck, Helmer Ringgren, and Heinz-Josef Fabry (eds), *Theological Dictionary of the Old Testament,* vol. 5 (Grand Rapids: Mich.: Eerdmans).

Long, V. Philips,

1999:   Israel's Past in Present research. Essays on Ancient Israelite Historiography (Sources for Biblical and Theological Study, vol. 7: Winona lake: Eisenbrauns).

Loretz, Oswald,

1984:   *Habiru-Hebräer. Eine sozio-linguistische Studie über die Herkunft des Gentiliziums ʿibrî vom Appellativum ḫabiru* (Beiheft zur *Zeitschrift für die alttestamentliche Wissenschaft,* 160; Berlin: Walter de Gruyter).

McKenzie, Steven L.,

2001:   "The Typology of the Davidic Covenant," pp. 152-178 in J. Andrew Dearman and M. Patrick Graham (eds), *The Land that I Will Show You. Essays on the History and Archaeology of the Ancient Near East in Honor of J. Maxwell Miller* (Journal for the Study of the Old Testament: Supplement Series, 343; Sheffield: Sheffield Academic Press).

Machinist, Peter,

1990:   "The Question of Distinctiveness in Ancient Israel," pp. 196-212 in M. Cogan and I. Eph'al (eds) *Ah, Assyria... Studies in Assyrian History and Ancient Near Eastern Historiography, Presented to Hayim Tadmor* (Scripta hierosolymitana; Jerusalem: The Magnes Press). [Reprinted, pp. 420-442 in Greenspahn 1991.]

Maidman, Maynard P.,

1995:   "Nuzi: Portrait of an Ancient Mesopotamian Provincial Town," pp. 931-947 in Sasson 1995.

Maier, Walter A., III,

1992:   "Anath (Deity)," *Anchor Bible Dictionary* (New York: Doubleday) 1: 225-227.

Malamat, Abraham,

1989:   *Mari and the Early Israelite Experience* (The Schweich Lectures of the British Academy, 1984; Oxford: Clarendon Press).

1998:   *Mari and the Bible* (Studies in the History and
             Culture of the Ancient Near East, 12; Leiden: Brill).

Margueron, Jean-Claude,
1992:   "Mari; Archaeology," *Anchor Bible Dictionary*
             (New York: Doubleday) 4: 525-529.

Meshel, Z.,
1992:   "Kuntillet ʿAjrud," *Anchor Bible Dictionary* (New
             York: Doubleday) 4: 103-109.
1994:   "Two Aspects in the Excavation of Kuntillet
             ʿAgrud," pp. 99-104 in Dietrich and Klopfenstein,
             1994.

Meyers, Carol L. and Eric M.,
1993:   *Zechariah 9-14. A New Translation with
             Introduction and Commentary* (The Anchor Bible,
             25c; New York: Doubleday).

Michalowski, Piotr,
1989:   *The Lamentation over the Destruction of Sumer
             and Ur* (Mesopotamian Civilizations, 1; Winona
             Lake, Ind.: Eisenbrauns).

Milano, Lucio,
1995:   "Ebla: A Third-Millennium City-State in Ancient
             Syria," pp. 1219-1230 in Sasson 1995.

Mollenkott, Virginia R.,

1983:   *The Divine Feminine: The Biblical Imagery of God as Female* (New York: Crossroad).

Moor, Johannes de,

1990:   *Rise of Yahwism: The Roots of Israelite Monotheism* (Bibliotheca ephemeridum theologicarum lovaniensium, 91; Leuven: Leuven University Press).

1986:   "The Crisis of Monotheism in Late Bronze Age Ugarit," *Oudtestamentische Studiën* 24: 1-20.

Moore, George F.,

1895:   *A Critical and Exegetical Commentary on Judges* (International Critical Commentary; Edinburgh: T. & T. Clark).

Moran, William,

1970:   "The Creation of Man in Atrahasis I 192-248," *Bulletin of the American Schools of Oriental Research* 200: 48-56.

Morrison, Martha A.,

1992:   "Nuzi," *Anchor Bible Dictionary* (New York: Doubleday) 4: 103-109.

Meek, Theophile J.,

1960:   *Hebrew Origins* (3rd edition; New York: Hebrew Origins).

Bibliography

Na'aman, Nadav,

2000: "Three Notes on the Aramaic Inscription from Tel Dan," *Israel Exploration Journal* 50: 92-104.

Nehmé, Laïla,

1999: *Guerre et conquête dans le Proche-Orient ancien. Actes de la table ronde du 14 1998 organisée par l'URA 1062 «Études Sémitiques»* (Antiquités Sémitiques, 4; Paris: J. Maisonneuve).

Niditch, Susan,

1987: *Underdogs and Tricksters. A Prelude to Biblical Folklore* (New York: Harper & Row).

Nissinen, Martti (ed),

2000: *Prophecy in Its Ancient Near Eastern Context: Mesopotamian, Biblical, and Arabian Perspectives* (SBL Symposium Series, 13; Atlanta: Society of Biblical Literature).

Norin, Stig,

1998: "The Age of the Siloam Inscription and Hezekiah's Tunnel," *Vetus Testamentum* 48: 37-48

Olender, Maurice,

1987: "The Indo-European Mirror: Monotheism and Polytheism," *History and Anthropology* 3: 327-374.

1992: *The Languages of Paradise: Race, Religion and Philology in the Nineteenth Century* (Cambridge: Harvard University Press).

Pardee, Dennis and Pierre Bordreuil,
1992:   "Ugarit, Texts and Literature" *Anchor Bible Dictionary* (New York: Doubleday) 6: 706-721.

Parpola, Simo,
2000:   "Monotheism in Ancient Assyria," pp. 165-209 in Porter 2000.

Poland, Lynn
1988:   "Defending Biblical Poetics," *Journal of Religion* 68: 426-434.

Pope, Maurice,
1999:   *The Story of Decipherment: From Egyptian Hieroglyphs to Maya Script* (Revised edition; London: Thames and Hudson).

Porter, Barbara Nevling,
2000:   *One God or Many. Concepts of Divinity in the Ancient World* (Transactions of the Casco Bay Assyriological Institute, 1; Chebeague Island, Mass.: CBAI).

Pritchard, James W.,
1969:   *Ancient Near Eastern Texts Relating to the Old Testament* (3rd edition; Princeton: Princeton University Press).

Bibliography

De Pury, Albert,

1992:   "Yahwist Source," *Anchor Bible Dictionary* (New York: Doubleday) 6: 1012-1020.

Rad, Gerhard von,

1991:   Holy War in Ancient Israel (Translated and edited by Marva J. Dawn and John H. Yoder; Grand Rapids, Mich.: Eerdmans).

Rainey, Anson F.,

2001a: "Stones for Bread. Archaeology versus History," *Near Eastern Archaeology* 64:140-149.

2001b: "Mesha and Syntax," pp. 287-307 in J. Andrew Dearman and M. Patrick Graham (eds), *The Land That I Will Show You. Essays on the History and Archaeology of the Ancient Near East in Honor of J. Maxwell Miller* (Journal for the Study of the Old Testament: Supplement Series, 343; Sheffield: Sheffield Academic Press).

Rogerson, J. W.,

1992:   "Interpretation, History of," *Anchor Bible Dictionary* (New York: Doubleday) 3: 425-433.

Ryan, William B. F. and Walter C. Pitman,

1999:   *Noah's Flood: The New Scientific Discoveries about the Event That Changed History* (New York: Simon & Schuster Inc.).

Sachs, Abe,

1976: "The Latest Datable Cuneiform Text," pp. 379-398 in Barry L. Eicher (ed), *Kramer Anniversary Volume. Cuneiform Studies in Honor of Samuel Noah Kramer* (Alter Orient und altes Testament 25; Kevelaer: Butzon & Bercker).

Saggs, H. W. F.,

1978: *The Encounter with the Divine in Mesopotamia and Israel* (London: The Athlone Press).

Sasson, Jack M.,

1966: "Circumcision in the Ancient Near East," *Journal of Biblical Literature* 85: 473-76.

1976: "Wordplay in the OT," *Interpreter's Dictionary of the Bible: Supplementary Volume* (Nashville: Abingdon), pp. 968-970.

1978: "A Genealogical 'Convention' in Biblical Chronography?" *Zeitschrift für die alttestamentlich Wissenschaft* 90: 171-85.

1984: "The Biographic Mode in Hebrew Historiography," pp. 305-312 in W. Boyd Barrick et al. (eds). *In the Shelter of Elyon. Essays on Ancient Palestinian Life and Literature in Honor of G. W. Ahlström* (Journal for the Study of the Old Testament: Supplement Series, 31; Sheffield: JSOT Press).

1992:   "Time ... to Begin," pp. 183-194 in M. Fishbane,
             E. Tov, and W. W. Fields(eds), *"Sha^carei Talmon":*
             Studies in the Bible, Qumran, and the Ancient
             Near East Presented to Shemaryahu Talmon
             (Winona Lake, Ind.: Eisenbrauns).

1995:   *Civilizations of the Ancient Near East* (4 vols; New
             York: Scribners and Sons; Republished in 2 vols,
             Peabody, Mass.: Henricksons, 2000).

1998:   "About 'Mari and the Bible'," *Revue*
             d'Assyriologie 92: 97-123.

Forthcoming: "The Image of Ancient Israel: Reacting to
             Presentations," forthcoming in *Text, Artifact, and*
             Image: Revealing Ancient Israelite Religion (Gary
             Beckman and Theodore J. Lewis, eds.

Forthcoming[2] "Origins and Media: Creation Narratives in the
             Ancient Israel and in Mesopotamia," in Lucien-
             Jean Bord & Piotr Skubiszewski (eds), *La Création,*
             liberté de dieu et liberté de l'homme dans les
             récits bibliques (Collection "La Tradition biblique";
             Paris: Cariscript).

Forthcoming[3] "Ritual Wisdom? On «Seething a Kid in its
             Mother's Milk»,": forthcoming contribution to a
             Festschrift.

Schmidt, Wilhelm,
1912:   *Der Ursprung der Gottesidee. Ein historisch-*
             kritisch und positiv Studie (Münster:
             Aschendorffsche Verlagsbuchhandlung).

van Seters, John,

1975: *Abraham in Tradition and History* (New Haven: Yale University Press).

Smelik, Klaas A. D.,

1991: *Writings from Ancient Israel. A Handbook of Historical and Religious Documents* (Louisville, Ky.: Westminster).

1992: *Converting the Past: Studies in the Ancient Israelite and Moabite Historiography* (Oudtestamentische Studiën, 27; Leiden: Brill).

Smith, George,

1874: "The Eleventh Tablet of the Izdubar Legends. The Chaldean Account of the Deluge," *Transactions of the Society of Biblical Archaeology* 3: 530-596

Smith, Mark S.,

2001a: *Untold Stories: The Bible and Ugaritic Studies in the Twentieth Century* (Peabody, Mass.: Hendrickson).

2001b: *The Origins of Biblical Monotheism: Israel's Polytheistic Background and the Ugaritic Texts* (New York: Oxford University Press).

van Soldt, Wilfred H.,

1995: "Ugarit: A Second-Millennium Kingdom on the Mediterranean Coast," pp. 1255-1266 in Sasson 1995.

Speiser, Ephraim A.,

1964: *Genesis. A New Translation with Introduction and Commentary* (The Anchor Bible, 1; New York: Doubleday).

Sperling, David,

1986: "Israel's Religion in the Ancient Near East," pp. 5-31 in Arthur Green (ed), *Jewish Spirituality. From the Bible through the Middle Ages* (World Spirituality, 13; New York: Crossroad).

Stern, Menahem,

2002: "The Babylonian Gap Revisited: Yes There Was," *Biblical Archaeology Review* 28/3: 39, 55.

Sternberg, Meir

1987: *The Poetics of Biblical Narrative* (Indiana Studies in Biblical Literature; Bloomington: Indiana University Press).

Stephens, Ferris J.,

1969: "Sumero-Akkadian Hymns and Prayers," pp. 383-392 in Pritchard 1969.

Tadmor, Hayim, B. Landsberger, and S. Parpola,

1989: "The Sin of Sargon and Sennacherib's Last Will," *State Archives of Assyria, Bulletin* 3: 1: 3-51.

Teller, James T, K. Glennie, N. Lancaster, and A. Singhvi,
2000:   "Calcareous Dunes of the United Arab Emirates
                and Noah's Flood; Post-glacial Reflooding of the
                Persian Gulf," *Quaternary International* 68-71:
                297-308.

Thompson, Thomas L.,
1974:   *The Historicity of the Patriarchal Narratives*
                (Beiheft zur *Zeitschrift für die alttestamentliche
                Wissenschaft*, 133; Berlin: Walter de Gruyter).

Tinney, Steve,
1996:   *The Nippur Lament* (Philadelphia: University of
                Pennsylvania Museum).

Toorn, Karel van der,
1992:   "Anat-Yahu, Some Other Deities, and the Jews of
                Elephantine," *Numen* 39: 80-101.

Vanderkam, James C.,
1995:   "Prophecy and Apocalyptics in the Ancient Near
                East," pp. 2083-2094 in Sasson 1995.

Vaux, Roland de,
1997:   *Ancient Israel. Its Life and Institutions* (The Biblical
                Resource Series; Grand Rapids, Mich.: Eerdmans).
1978:   *The Early History of Israel* (Philadelphia:
                Westminster Press).

Veenhof, Klaas,

1990:   "De interpretatie van de Atrachasis-mythe, een Babylonische oergeschiedenis," *Nederlands theologisch tijdschrift* 44: 77-197.

1995-96:   "The Old Assyrian hamushtum-period: a seven-day week," Jaarbericht van het Vooraziatisch - Egyptisch Gezelschap 'ExOriente Lux' 34: 5-26.

Vermes, Geza,

1998:   *The Complete Dead Sea Scrolls in English* (London: Penguin Books).

De Vries, Simon J.,

1962:   "Chronology of the Old Testament," *Interpreter's Dictionary of the Bible* (Nashville: Abingdon) 1: 580-599.

1976:   "Chronology, OT," *Interpreter's Dictionary of the Bible: Supplementary Volume* (Nashville: Abingdon), pp. 162-166.

Weinfeld, Moshe,

1970:   "The Covenant of Grant in the Old Testament and in the Ancient Near East," *Journal of the American Oriental Society* 90: 184-203.

1991:   *Deuteronomy 1-11. A New Translation with Introduction and Commentary* (The Anchor Bible, 5; New York: Doubleday).

Weippert, Manfred,

1976-80:   "Jahwe," *Reallexikon der Assyriologie* 5: 246-253.

Wente, Edward F.,

2000:   "Monotheism," Oxford Encyclopedia of Ancient Egypt (New York: Oxford University Press) 3: 432-435.

Wesselius, Jan-Wim,

2001:   "Collapsing the Narrative Bridge," pp. 247-255 in J. W. Dyk et al.(eds), *"Unless some one guide me ...": Festschrift for Karel A. Deurloo* (Amsterdamse Cahiers voor Exegese van de Bijbel en zijn Tradities: Supplement, 2; Masstricht: Shaker).

White, Hayden,

1980:   "The Value of Narrativity," *Critical Inquiry* 7: 8-17.

Whiting, Robert M.

1995:   "Amorite Tribes and Nations of Second-Millennium Western Asia," pp. 1231-1242 in Sasson 1995.

Wiggins, Steve A.,

2001:   "Of Asherahs and Trees: Some Methodological Questions," *Journal of Ancient Near Eastern Religions* 1: 158-187.

Williams, Ronald,

1970: "The Passive *qal* Theme in Hebrew," pp. 43-50 in J. W. Wevers and D. B. Redford (eds), *Essays on the Ancient Semitic World* (Toronto: University of Toronto Press).

Wilson, Robert R.,

1992: "Genealogy, Genealogies," *Anchor Bible Dictionary* (New York: Doubleday) 2: 929-932.

Würthwein, Ernst,

1979: *The Text of the Old Testament* (Grand Rapids, Mich.: Eerdmans).

Yon, Marguerite,

1992: "Ugarit, History and Archaeology," *Anchor Bible Dictionary* (New York: Doubleday) 6: 999-1008. (New York: Doubleday) 6: 695-706.

Zevit, Ziony,

2002: "Three Debates about Bible and Archaeology," *Biblica* 83: 1-27.

General Index

General Index

Gospel Writing and Church Politics : *A Socio-rhetorical Approach*

Chuen King Lecture Series 3 (216 pages) US$15/£10
Gerd Theissen (Heidelberg University)

The aim of this book is to demonstrate the social function of the Gospels and Acts in their historical context. The Gospels do not only tell and describe the life and teaching of Jesus, they are also to influence their audience to shape Christian life in the earliest Christian communities.

Jesus, Paul and John Chuen King Lecture Series 1 (175 pages) US$12/£8

C.K Barrett "The Development of Theology in the New Testament"
A.J. Malherbe "The Apostle Paul as a Pastor"
Kosuke Koyama "Towards Human Picture Theology—The Use of Bible in Contextualizing Theology"

Nowadays in Asian churches, including Chinese Christian communities, one of the main concerns is to contextualize Christian theologies, which have been developed in the West for almost two thousand years in their own contexts...

We believe that we can learn from Western biblical scholars their study of what Scripture meant in their original contexts, and try our effort to understand the messages in our own contexts.

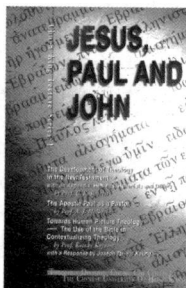

Paul's Purpose in Writing Romans (536 pages Hard Cover) US$38/£25

Lung-kwong LO (The Chinese University of Hong Kong)

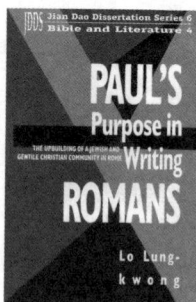

"A major problem with earlier treatments of Romans which have attempted to clarify the situation in Rome and the purpose of the letter, however, has failed to correlate the epistolary framework and final ethical section with the main body and doctrinal core of the Epistle. This is where the present volume adds significantly to the contemporary debate. The author has developed a fresh method of analysis by focusing on the use of first and second persons, which is surprisingly simple, but which has achieved some very interesting and persuasive results. And his exegesis highlights links in the argument of the letter which have not been noticed before and have not been given sufficient attention."

James D. G. Dunn

Interpretations of Hope in Chinese Religions and Christianity

Christian Study Centre on Chinese Religion and Culture (290 pages Paper Back) USD16/£12
Daniel L. OVERMYER and Chi-tim LAI, Editors

Hope represents a universal quest of the human race. It is a concern for and speculation of one's own future. The emergence of any form of religions was closely related to that human quest. This book is the fruit of an outstanding group of Asian and Western scholars' studies on the notion of "hope" in Chinese Religions, namely Confucianism, Taoism and Buddhism, as well as in Christianity. It aims at setting a platform for the dialogue between Chinese and Western Religions, and widening the reader's horizon to understand the human quest of hope from different historical, and cultural perspectives.

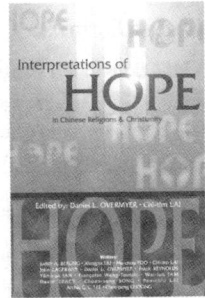

Ching Feng (first published under the title Quarterly Notes in 1957)

Christian Study Centre on Chinese Religion and Culture

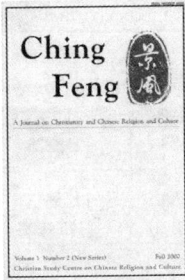

This is a bi-annual journal published by The principal aim of Ching Feng is to promote critical investigation into all aspects of Chinese Christianity, Chinese Religions, and Inter-religious Dialogue between Christianity and Asian Religions. Ching Feng welcomes innovative papers which seek to develop critical perspectives on these three areas, especially those that work across traditional disciplinary boundaries, or those that deal with a methodological critique of accepted academic conceptualizations.

JTCA (The Journal of Theologies and Cultures in Asia)

PTCA (The Programme for Theology and Cultures in Asia)

It is an annual journal published by the PTCA, offers a forum for exploring the Asian ways of doing theology. The PTCA was founded in 1983, it is not an organization nor an institution but a theological movement, and committed to: 1. helping equip theologians and church leaders in a theological reorientation for their various ministries; 2. recovering our own cultural and spiritual resources in Asian countries and making these available for the doing of living theologies in Asia; 3. promoting creative, indigenous theological writing within the concrete experiences and heritages of the Asia arena and 4. facilitating active theological interactions within Asia and between Asia and other parts of the world.

ORDER FORM

Name of Individual / Institution: _____

Address:_____

Fax:_____ Email:_____

Order Details:

THEOLOGY DIVISION, CHUNG CHI COLLEGE

TITLE	ISBN	QTY	UNIT PRICE	TOTAL
Gospel Writing and Church Politics: A Socio-rhetorical Approach	962-7137-29-4		US$15 / £10	
Jesus, Paul and John	962-7137-21-9		US$12 / £8	
Paul's Purpose in Writing Romans	962-7997-27-7		US$38 / £25	

CHRISTIAN STUDY CENTRE ON CHINESE RELIGION AND CULTURE

TITLE	ISBN	QTY	UNIT PRICE	TOTAL
Interpretations of Hope in Chinese Religions and Christianity	962-7706-04-3		US$16 / £12	

Subscription Rates: *Ching Feng* (ISSN: HK0009 4668)

ONE-YEAR SUBSCRIPTION (2 issues)	☐ US$43 / £12 (seamail)	☐ US$45 / £13 (airmail)
SINGLE COPY	☐ US$22 / £6 (seamail)	☐ US$23 / £6.5 (airmail)

Subscription Rates: *JTCA* (ISSN: 1682-6086)

Area	1 yr.	2 yr.	3 yr.
Asia, Australia, New Zealand, Pacific Island States, Africa, Latin America	☐ US$12	☐ US$23	☐ US$33
Canada, Europe, USA and others	☐ US$18	☐ US$34	☐ US$48
Hong Kong	☐ HK$75	☐ HK$140	☐ HK$200

Note: The above listed prices include surface mail, handling and bank charges.

Payment Details:

☐ Cheque enclosed for US$/£_____ payable for **CHUNG CHI COLLEGE**

☐ Cheque enclosed for US$/£_____ payable for *"Christian Study Centre on Chinese Religion and Culture"*

☐ Please send me an invoice

Send to:

1. **Purchase order or Subscription order** on Theology Division and Christian Study Centre on Chinese Religion and Culture, please send to Theology Building, Chung Chi College, The Chinese University of Hong Kong, Shatin, New Territories, HONG KONG
2. **Subscription on *JTCA***: *All subscriptions should be directed to Mans' Book Company (email:info@mansbook.com)*

Contact:

(852)-2609 6711(Tel.) or (852)-2603 5224 (Fax) or theology@cuhk.edu.hk (Email)
Please allow 4-6 weeks for overseas delivery.